SCARED OF YOUR BOSS?

SMASH THROUGH YOUR FEAR

NOW!

SIGNE A. DAYHOFF, PHD

Scared of Your Boss?
Smash Through Your Fear Now!
By Signe A. Dayhoff, PhD

Published by Effectiveness-Plus Publications LLC
80 Paseo de San Antonio
Placitas, New Mexico 87043-8735

Cover image @Fotosearch.com.

Design by around86
and ilgeorgiev at fiverr.com

ISBN: 978-0-9985324-2-4

PUBLISHER'S NOTE

TABLE OF CONTENTS

§ § §

INTRODUCTION

§ § §

Meet the people you will be following as they each deal with a different workplace fear of authority.

FRANK – A heavy-set, balding, middle-aged man with ham-like hands, piercing blue eyes, and a bulldog jaw, Frank was an imposing figure as he walked the floor of the automotive assembly plant in Huntsville, Alabama. When workers first saw their new supervisor, striding around, unsmiling, they did double-takes. Because of the way he carried himself, they could picture him on a Hog tearing up the asphalt, riding with the Hell's Angels through California desert towns.

But while he looked like "it's my way or the highway," Frank had no sense of his own authority. Even worse, he felt powerless to make suggestions, relate problems, or deal in anyway with anyone in authority, such as management. In their presence he was submissively stooped over with his head down.

TASHA - Twenty-five, short, and athletic, Tasha, who wore her modified Afro with pride, was a computer program designer with a glowing track record and an acknowledged bright future. She had risen quickly in the ranks at Silicon Valley communications companies. She was sought after.

Yet despite her educational achievements and in-demand professional design work, she saw herself as inadequate to the job, skipping meetings when she could so as not to be under the up-close scrutiny of her boss. Subconsciously she was always concerned that she would be found out and seen as the "fake" she "knew" she really was.

STEFAN - Tall and slim with a slight accent, dark-haired, olive-complexioned, Stefan was a twenty-six-year-old, freshly-minted physician—the pride of his Old-World parents. As they had hoped and pushed, he had successfully made his way through a prestigious school of medicine in Massachusetts. He was interning in an old, well-respected Boston hospital that boasted many well-known senior teaching physicians in residence.

One thing Stefan had learned throughout his years in education and training was that one *never* questions the judgment of senior doctors ... no matter what. You kept your mouth shut in the presence of authority and power. You thought twice before raising your hand. To do otherwise was to do so at your peril. Quaking at the mere thought, Stefan always pictured himself as "A Tale of Two Cities" Sydney Carton taking Charles Darnay's place on a rickety tumbril on his way to the guillotine.

Most of us have experienced some degree of fear of an authority figure at some time, such as a boss, parent, teacher, police officer, etc. A recent poll on workplace fears conducted by CareerBuilder found that 26 percent of workers reported that they feared their bosses; 18 percent stated they feared presenting in front of their bosses; and 11 percent stated they feared meeting executives—all forms of social anxiety which some have termed as "boss phobia."

In looking at those low numbers, one needs to keep in mind that admitting to fearing one's boss is a socially undesirable behavior—something most would prefer not to do, irrespective of the degree to which they may have experienced that fear.

According to British journalist Russell H. Ewing, fear of bosses is anything but uncommon.

The difference between a "boss" and a "leader" is quite striking, demonstrating why fear of a boss is likely to exist. He suggests "a boss creates fear, a leader confidence. A boss fixes blame, a leader corrects mistakes. A boss knows all, a leader asks questions. A boss makes work drudgery, a leader makes it interesting." As he points out, unfortunately there are more bosses around than leaders.

While this description of "bosses" is a generalization, there have been and are enough bosses—individuals more interested in control and power than in interpersonally sensitive and productive management—around who fit the description to foster fear as a result. These findings are supported by the work of psychologists and coaches Dr. Herbert Rappaport at Temple University, Dr. John Weaver of Psychology for Business, and Dick Schubert of Executive Coaching Network, Inc. who work with business supervisors, managers, executives, and leaders.

This fear of any authority figure, or specifically one's boss, may have appeared to you as a momentary feeling of panic in some situation. Perhaps you wondered if you had done something wrong. Had you disobeyed someone, broken a social or business rule, not spoken up when you should have, or not done a good job on your latest task? This feeling may have lasted for only a day or a few weeks until you acclimated to the particular new job. Or, it may have become a seemingly "permanent" concern whenever and wherever you worked.

In any of these authority-fear situations you likely felt self-conscious, unassertive, and lacking any sense of personal control at that time. Ever-present in your thinking were those anxiety-provoking "shoulds": what you *should* do, what you *should* have done, what you *should not* do, what you *should* not have done. "Shoulds" are directives, rules, regulations, laws, and guides designed by the powers-that-be to make sure you do what cultural, social, governmental, legal, or business authorities want you to do. To do otherwise is to challenge authority for which there is some kind of punishment.

In these authority-fear situations you are always a little on edge about what authority figures might think about you. That is, you fear that you would be negatively evaluated if you drew attention to yourself, spoke up, asked questions, made suggestions, or made a social, business, or work error. You fear the consequence of being seen as inadequate or a miscreant: being humiliated, rejected, or even fired.

Irrespective of how, when, and where you experienced this fear of authority figures, it made you and your situation uncomfortable, perhaps even depressingly miserable, as you worried about not finding a way you could comfortably adapt.

My own research, coaching, and consulting over the past thirty-five-plus years have shown me that many people, both professionals and non-professionals, share some degree of this fear of bosses or those in authority—both in and out of the workplace. Because of individuals' earlier life experiences, fear of authority figures in some form is nearly a universal. While some expressions of that fear may seem trivial, when that fear occurs in the workplace, it can be devastating because of its potential negative consequences and implications for your career, finances, and self-esteem.

The following program helps you smash through that challenging fear. You replace that fear with vibrant self-confidence and assertiveness. You feel empowered as you face your fears, stand up to them, and conquer them so you can achieve your goals.

This master program is a graduated course which consists of three (3) sequential 3-week Stepping Stones. Each Stepping Stone represents a stage or level you need to master and then pass through. Each helps you determine, secure, maintain, and manifest your strengths, interpersonal skills, and confidence as a person and a worker.

The three sequential 3-week course levels are Stepping Stone I (Basic), Stepping Stone II (Intermediate), and Stepping Stone III (Advanced). Together they will help you achieve your authority-related goals:

- Understanding and dealing with authority
- Gaining people- and communication skills and self-esteem
- Deep-sixing your fear of your boss
- Standing up for yourself in a respectful manner
- Speaking comfortably with authority figures and bosses.

Discovering and believing in your strengths and successes is essential for your building confidence in interacting with your boss and other authority figures. Consequently, the course will show you the resources you possess as a human being and employee and the unique value you offer to others in the workplace. It will help you build your confidence in those resources.

Furthermore, it will provide you with the proven, practical thinking and behavioral skills necessary to uncover and overcome your fear. This will allow you to deal comfortably and effectively with any authority figures. As a Japanese proverb says, "Fear is only as deep as the mind allows."

This program is based on addressing the three primary components, or building blocks, of your fear: the Cognitive (what you think and the reasons behind it), Emotional (how you feel as a result), and Physiological (how your body responds to those thoughts and emotions). Because each of these factors contributes to and reinforces your fear, you will discover how to master each one through numerous, proven, step-by-step strategies and techniques.

Then the program will help you replace ineffective, negative thought, beliefs, and behavior habits with effective, positive thoughts, beliefs, and behavior habits. Finally, it will help you put it all together so that you can see authority for what it really is. It will melt your resistance, overcome your roadblocks, and increase your confidence, assertiveness, and competence in the workplace and any other place wherein authorities may dwell.

Overall, you'll learn:

1. What your strengths are
2. What authority really means and how to respond to it effectively
3. How you and your boss are similar and dissimilar as people and role holders
4. Where your resistances and roadblocks that hold you back may reside
5. How to relax to de-stress yourself before, during, and after anxiety-provoking situations
6. How to step back from your automatic fear emotions to look at your boss objectively, test the reality of your negative thoughts, and firmly dispute them
7. How your past and present successes redefine your abilities and achievements
8. How expectation and preparation create confidence and empowerment

9. How to praise and reward every small thing you do right to make your achievements stick like glue
10. How you can prepare to successfully speak and interact with your boss, and other authority figures, and feel good about it and yourself.

HOW DOES THIS FEAR COME ABOUT?

§ § §

Before you start on the course, you need to understand where your fear of authority figures may come from. You've had a glimpse at *Frank*, *Tasha*, and *Stefan*'s authority problems. You need to know where they can originate. Likewise, you need to have an understanding of how that fear can impact and has impacted your life, other than just making you feel anxious, miserable, and depressed. What this means is you need to begin by defining and dissecting the concept of the "authority figure."

An "authority figure" is someone who has been given the power to tell you what to do. Along with this, he or she has been given the ability and discretion to threaten and punish you in some way if you don't do what they dictate. According to social psychologist and psychoanalyst Erich Fromm, "Authority is not a quality one person 'has,' in the sense that he has property or physical qualities. Authority is an interpersonal relation in which one person looks upon another as somebody superior to him."

As mentioned earlier, an authority figure can be a parent, guardian, teacher, business owner, client or customer, boss, physician, lawyer, police officer, minister/priest/rabbi/imam, judge, and other elected or appointed official, for example. In most instances, this individual has this power because society, some individual or group of individuals, citizens, organization, institution, or government has given it to that person by virtue of the roles she or he possesses and acts on.

How you relate to authority depends upon your perception of and expectations about it. As a child, you were taught to respect and obey authority. As a result, you have buried in your brain the requirement to respond "appropriately" to this authority regarding the things you *should* do and the things you *should not* do. This leaves a lingering subconscious fear about doing something you have been told not to do. It presents itself as *anxiety before* and *guilt after* you transgress some societal norm, moral principle, law, rule, regulation, or order.

Frank's perception of and expectations about authority stemmed from his father. When Frank was a small, scrawny child, his father constantly maligned him for being stupid, weak, and unwilling to stand up for himself. His father repeatedly told him he should "man up" and never back away from a confrontation. Bullied at school for his size and reluctance to fight, he finally snapped and began to strike back at his more developed combatants, but without much success. He still felt inadequate.

Tasha's came from her minister and from the family environment that placed authority in the hands of their religion. Always lurking in the inner recesses of her mind was what her minister had long proclaimed she *should* do with her life. No matter how much she was attracted to and excelled at computer sciences and design, he stated she should commit and devote her life to helping her community through activism. Fighting for social, political, and economic justice was the way he knew she could best serve God. He praised how people responded to her and that she was a go-getter. And now she spent much of her time fretting about being discovered in her current "masquerade."

Stefan's concern with authority came from his always having placed medical professionals on a tall pedestal. In their god-like position whatever they dictated was law and physicians-to-be had to be aware and carefully follow their dictates, or else. One day during grand rounds he made an "error" in asking a simple question of their physician instructor. As a result, the physician sneered at him and made him look like a ludicrous public spectacle. Scathingly he shot Stefan down as a "pathetic ignoramus who was barely suited to scooping elephant droppings from the grounds at the Franklin Park Zoo." Abashed and red-faced, Stefan was disinclined to ever do it again—certainly not when he knew a single miffed, all-powerful physician could ruin his chances of ever getting a good job anywhere.

Consider for a minute how you felt as a kid in school when you were caught and publicly admonished by your teacher for doing something that didn't meet the teacher's expectations, such as, being late, talking in class, chewing gum, passing notes, or casually glancing at your friend's test paper. Chances are good you were left with a bad feeling in the pit of your stomach. That was your conscience saying "Uh-oh, I *shouldn't* have done that!" (And, perhaps, "I shouldn't have gotten caught!") Even when the teacher misperceived or misunderstood your actions, you anxiously wondered what was going to happen to you as a result.

Or consider how you feel now when you are driving and a police car suddenly appears behind you in your rearview mirror. There is likely an automatic surge of adrenaline that not only races your heart but also lifts your foot from the accelerator. Your mind is likely to ponder, "What's the problem? Uh-oh, what did I do?"

Whenever you hear yourself talking about "shoulds," you're talking about some norm, principle, law, regulation, rule, or order that some "authority" has dictated you *need* to follow ... or else. Consequently, "shoulds" tend to make you anxious and fearful because of the possibility of your consciously or unconsciously not adhering to them. Often that feeling is negatively reinforced by a bad childhood experience with these "shoulds."

WHAT CONTRIBUTES TO THIS FEAR?

§ § §

There are four (4) negative categories of experience which can contribute to your fear of authority figures.

1. *Strict, critical or overbearing parents or guardians* who made you feel inadequate and powerless to do anything *other than* as they dictated you should. No matter what you did, it likely did not get their full approval of being "acceptable" to them. There was always something "wrong."

This was *Frank*'s father. When Frank could no longer take the bullying from classmates, he tried to "man-up" as his father commanded and fight for himself. Unfortunately, it was Frank alone who was inevitably caught and reprimanded by teachers for fighting on school grounds and, as they claimed, "acting like a hooligan."

Being caught meant an accusing call from the principal to his father that Frank was a "major disruptive force in school." But to his father

Frank's not winning the fights was worse than his not obeying school rules. Moreover, being called to the principal's office would anger and embarrass his father. Then there was the question of whether Frank would be suspended or expelled. So, when Frank was called to the principal's office, he knew he was in for several dressings down—and all because he tried to do what he was "should" do according to the authority figure that mattered most to him.

2. *Overly-cautious parents* who were overly concerned about protecting you from potential dangers, including the consequences and implications of not abiding by laws and what society expected. They continually admonished you to be careful. This suggested that the world was a threatening, dangerous place where you had to be on guard about your safety.

3. *Conditioned response to some authority figure* who made you to feel negatively evaluated, judged, and rendered powerless over time.

Every time *Tasha*'s boss came near, she froze. She was certain he would see that she should really be doing what her minister had dictated she should do. Controlling her fate, her boss could act on his inner knowledge of her façade and fire her. She knew he could hear the ringing voice of her minister telling her she "shouldn't" follow her own career desires. This meant she had to be perfect to keep her boss distracted from detecting her true self and act on her impersonation.

4. *Traumatic incident involving a person in authority* who publicly embarrassed, humiliated, rejected, or punished you for some perceived infraction.

Stefan knew reputation was everything in the profession of medicine. He also knew that medicine was political, where good connections and good relations mattered above all, sometimes even before expertise and experience. Ill-feelings of senior physicians never disappeared. They were inscribed in some universal account ledger to be resurrected at any time against another.

During his rotation in the chaotic emergency room, a senior doctor confused two patients and reversed their treatment recommendations. Stefan had just been looking at the patients' charts. He saw that diagnoses and treatments didn't match. But what should he do? He couldn't correct the charts himself and he didn't dare ask the senior a question about the assigned treatments. That would be like accusing the senior of making a serious error. He could feel his stomach juices churn.

WHAT ABOUT HIGH STATUS?

§ § §

Because of its accompanying authority and associated sense of "superiority," high status is something you also consciously *and* unconsciously concern yourself with. High status likewise has requirements for what you *should* do and *should not do* with respect to those who have it. The higher the status one has the greater the requirements there are for you to show respect when interacting with or merely being around that person. High status in every society is thought to have some acknowledged social value. High status can represent *social* status, *financial* status, *business* status, *professional* status, *celebrity* status, *sports* status, *artistic* status, *educational* status, and *political* status.

Generally, it is through social comparisons that you and everyone else naturally determine and evaluate your own personal status, power, and authority in your individual circumstances. You do it to see how you compare with specific higher status others on factors such as *success*, *wealth*, *attractiveness*, *education*, *privilege*, *job*, *pay*, *job perks*, *abilities*, *experience*, *interests*, *associations*, *relationships*, *freedoms of action*, and *talents*.

You compare yourself to see if you are in sync with the expectations of your society, the culture, a group or individual you value, or with specific beliefs and attitudes you consider important. You do it to see how you are similar to those you admire or *dissimilar* to those you don't like and devalue. You do it to see what you might do to make yourself more like those you admire—more acceptable, accepted, and valued.

However, not all social comparisons are positive or useful. Depending upon your history with how you learned you "should" think, act, and feel about others with high status and in authority, you may have very negative feelings about those who can exert their status and power over you. You may resent them as well as fear them. Social comparisons, in such cases, do not help you decide how you'd like to advance in some area and how to do it. Instead, they can block you, creating big problems for you.

When you are not using these comparisons to *positively enhance* your behavior to achieve your goals, you are likely using them instead to irrationally point out possible "inadequacies" in yourself. Negative comparisons, in general but especially with one's boss, create anger, a sense of powerlessness, low self-esteem, and maladaptive thoughts, feelings, and behaviors—things that can get in your way in your personal and work lives.

In the workplace negative comparisons with anyone seen to have authority can affect your level of productivity, mood, interpersonal interactions, and make you vulnerable to the authority's use of the power that you fear. Having to obey or respond to them in a formalized and "inequitable" manner, you will tend to see authorities as being treated as more entitled because of their status and you as less entitled by comparison. This helps keep your fear of authority figures, and your resulting anger, alive and well.

Frank, now found that just having to speak to his superiors at work made him choke up, sweat, and feel nauseous. He even experienced his neck muscles tightening when having to speak with workers who had been employed at the plant for a long time.

Tasha "knew" the next time her boss approached her, he would demand some task she couldn't perform and she would be publicly humiliated. It was getting worse. Everything her boss said to her she was interpreting as lurking criticism. Even when he lavished praise on her for her program design creativity, she cringed, and waited for the other shoe to drop.

Stefan knew telling the physician about the ER patients' mistake would be another loud, public disparagement of his person and medical abilities, as well as another black mark on his record. While he wouldn't get off as "easily" as the last time he spoke up, it would be lots worse for the patients if he didn't. "First do no harm" raced through his mind. He felt disoriented, fearful of sabotaging himself, caught in a damned-if-you-do and damned-if-you-don't dilemma.

Fortunately for Stefan, at that moment another physician happened to check the charts, discovered the mistake, and corrected it. He had been saved ... as had the two patients ... *this* time ... but felt sick physically and emotionally about it. What was he going to do next time when someone didn't happen to be there to save him? He couldn't let a patient die.

AUTHORITY" IS A LABEL

§ § §

To understand how your fear of authority figures plays out in the workplace (and anywhere else) you have to put authority figures into perspective. You do that by personally dissecting and re-assessing the label of "authority" and how you respond to it. This means specifically

1. Digging beneath the label, role, or job title
2. Objectively evaluating what perceptions, suppositions, and expectations are there
3. Removing the "label's" emotional power.

Your perception of the label of authority or high status (social, business, financial, professional, celebrity, artistic, sports, educational, or political) comes from what you learned to accept in childhood that was continuously reinforced by society. In general, you learned that any person who has that label has the right to judge your actions AND has the right to use their associated power to act against you if you don't follow the accepted "shoulds." You may worry that authorities around you may use their power without your best interests at heart.

According to philosopher Bertrand Russell, "Worry is a form of fear and all forms of fear produce fatigue." As a result, when you worry about or fear your boss, you may feel depressed, one-down, angry, and impotent. You may feel you have to act somewhat submissively or defensively to protect yourself from that power, which, in turn, tends to breed doubt about yourself and more fear. It also likely affects how the authority figure perceives you, for good or ill.

In the workplace your anxiety may be associated with being humiliated or a fear of losing your job through that person's use of their power. Feeling at risk is often frightening and demoralizing. It is important to note, however, that while people with authority may have the "power" to fire you, in general their actually doing so has a very low probability of happening. That is aside from the occurrence of specific situations such as mergers, down-sizing, a recessionary economy, a political power grab, your flagrantly flouting authority, or your becoming unproductive.

Titles and roles of authority figures are merely "labels" that are *assigned* to certain people in certain roles in order for them to accomplish certain tasks. There is nothing inherently special about someone who has that label except in the marketplace. In many cases the *real* differences between you and your boss, e.g., are only that you

1. Work on slightly different paths
2. Use slightly different approaches to tasks
3. Have slightly different responsibilities toward task achievement
4. Receive slightly different compensation for those responsibilities.

One of the most important things you need to do is mentally *erase* that individual's authority or high-status *label*. You need to see them as a *person* first and in a *particular role* second. You would still need to respect their title or role by adhering to any accompanying role expectations of behavior, attitude, and respect. But when you interact with them, you would concentrate on what you need to do to speak with and interact with them in order to achieve your goal. As Babe Ruth said, "Never let fear of striking out get in your way."

Why is it so important for you to disengage from their label? Consider what happens to you behaviorally when you experience that fear. Your performance suffers because your thoughts and emotions are focused on worrying about being evaluated negatively and wondering how you can survive it.

When your thoughts are not focused on your being a positive, productive employee, you cannot effectively focus on your being the professional and team member your boss and the company want you to be. After all, how could you concentrate on your doing your best when you constantly feel the need to

1. Analyze everything that happens on the job
2. Spend your time fretting about what your boss's behavior means *now*
3. Negatively anticipate what it may mean in your *future.*

Consequently, when you allow yourself to be anxiously distracted, it isn't long before you begin to feel hypervigilant and hypersensitive. You monitor what your boss says and does with respect to your value, effort, and position at work. You tend to focus on negatively comparing yourself to your fellow employees' work efforts, their results, and how the boss responds to them.

You can see how these negative thoughts and feelings would be very harmful to your emotional and work health. This means you need to *immediately* call a halt to them, like putting up a large red mental STOP sign. If you let them continue, they will lurk in the back of your mind, tainting your every work thought, action, feeling, and interaction. They *will* sabotage you unless you find ways to eliminate them.

YOU ARE A DIFFERENT LABEL

§ § §

What all this further suggests is that you need to totally re-assess how you see yourself. That is, you need to see the *real* you—not the one you have negatively focused on as a result of your negative social comparisons and authority fears.

When you can step outside your current mindset of being one-down because you are not the "powerful authority," you can discover that despite your fearful emotions and negative thoughts, you are really a responsible, conscientious, productive, talented, and valuable professional. As such, you are highly *unlikely* to create a real circumstance in which you'd be seen as inadequate or fired.

You'll see that you actually *have power* but just a different kind of power from that of your boss. To do this you will assess your strengths, positive attributes, behaviors, expertise, and experiences in *all* the aspects of your life. These aspects include your *work life*, *personal life*, *family*, and *community*.

You will compare yourself in the present with yourself in the past on these strengths, attributes, and other factors. Knowing your strengths and successes, you can emerge from your fear cocoon and assume your real, underlying positive and motivated work personality. You can see yourself as conquering fear, becoming action-oriented, and producing confidence and courage.

As you work on your fear thoughts, feelings, and behaviors, you will reveal your positive strengths and your growth and development, which you have likely overlooked to date because of your fear. Feeling fear tends to submerge, discount, and dismiss your positive attributes as well as your past and present successes. Seeing yourself positively is ultra-important for you to enhance your self-esteem, self-confidence, and alleviate your fear. As you see yourself positively, you will see authority figures and those with high status as human beings arbitrarily possessing *different* labels and roles from you.

When you re-assess and work on your positive strengths and attributes, you build on them. Specifically, you can use them in your workplace to make yourself a better and more confident employee (and person). As you discover these positive strengths and attributes, you will also begin to remember success instances as well. These success instances will point to the fact that you have already acted positively, productively, and effectively. They will provide concrete, specific proof that you are anything but inadequate in any circumstance at work or elsewhere. Furthermore, these success instances will point out that you have the wherewithal—your own power—to go after more of the things you want and achieve them.

As you smash through your fear of authorities via these three Stepping Stones, you will learn how to minimize your fears and maximize your strengths and successes, as you will see Frank, Tasha, and Stefan doing it. You will gain a new perspective on authority, what it means and doesn't mean. You will discover how to reinforce everything positive and important you do, and have done (no matter how small), with praise and reward. Ultimately you can see yourself as the valuable, confident resource you are. If you're ready, let's begin!

STEPPING STONE I– WEEK #1

§ § §

Before you can begin to deal with your fear of your boss—or any authority figure—you need a clear and accurate understanding of what an authority figure is. So, we're all on the same page, we'll use the following definition. An "authority figure" is someone who is *given the power to tell you what to do and not to do.* As a result, this is one who expects you to do what it tells you to do.

This is one who *can* punish you in some way if you don't do it. Moreover, this is one who *can* praise and reward you if you do. You need to keep in mind that *can* doesn't necessarily mean *will* ... and there's *no* reason to assume it one way or the other.

To reiterate: An authority figure can be a parent, teacher, religious leader, business owner, professional, boss, law officer, elected or appointed official, or judge, for example. In most instances, their power came through its being bestowed upon them by society, some individual, some group of individuals, an organization, the government, or institution. Authority is a part of the role the authority figure holds and plays.

As a child, you were taught to respect some type of authority ... or suffer the consequences. The result of this is a lingering anxiety about your potentially transgressing some societal principle, rule, or law.

Authority is based on "shoulds" ... and "shoulds" tend to set up roadblocks and make you fearful. But these "shoulds" don't apply *only* to authority figures. They also apply to those with high status. High status can come from those with high social, financial, business, professional, celebrity, artistic, educational, or political standing. Status is something you consciously and unconsciously concern yourself with because it has accompanying power as well as dos and don'ts.

Note: Before we go on, one of the first things you need to do as you start this program is to create a *Daily Log* for yourself in which to Record your Observations, Answer Exercise Questions, and note your daily progress by answering your Progress Report questions. This is a *necessity.*

What works best for this is a three-ring 8 ½" x 11" loose leaf binder. You can add information about yourself, your daily experiences with fear of your boss, what you do for practice, the results you received from your practice, and weekly graphs that chart your stepping-stone progress.

The three-ring notebook gives you the flexibility of adding, deleting, and re-arranging information etc. by sections using section tags of different colors.

Be Sure to Record ALL Fear Experiences, Exercises and Your Responses in Your Daily Log

EXERCISE –*Your Relationship to Authority*

1. Write down <u>one</u> societal principle, rule, or law you have been expected to obey.
2. Write down <u>one</u> "should" in your *work* life.
3. Write down an early negative experience you had with some authority figure.
4. Write down a high-status person to whom you compare yourself favorably.
5. Write down a high-status person to whom you compare yourself negatively.
6. Write down who gave or assigned the title, role, and power to your boss.

7. Write down under what circumstances *you* might have been given or assigned the title, role, and power your boss currently has.
8. Write down an instance at work when you were focusing more on your boss and less on your work. What happened and how did you feel?
9. Write down an instance where you experienced hypersensitivity to something your boss said or did because of your fear of what an authority might do to you.
10. Write down one success (large or small) you have had at work.

When you fear your boss, you tend to feel inadequate in some way with respect to that person and your shared work situation. This sense of "inadequacy" becomes a roadblock. It tends to minimize your perception of your worth as an employee, as compared with your boss, and/or other employees.

This means you are not seeing the value of your resources, experience, and expertise. Instead you are focusing on your "failures" or "lacks." When you do this, you are not recognizing the many positive attributes you have and the successes you have had over the years, since you were a child. This creates a negative mindset which interferes with your seeing who you really are, what you have achieved, and what you *can* achieve.

Now you will look at what is positive about you, specifically at your attributes. Your attributes include your character, abilities, skills, talents, expertise, experience, values, appearance, connections, knowledge areas, education, intelligence, social effectiveness, and thinking, emotional, physical, and spiritual strengths.

You likely have been not fully aware of all you have going for you. This means you need to be reminded of all the positive and useful resources you already have. You will rediscover and look at these attributes in both your past and present. You need to look at both past and present because the degree, extent, and quality of your personal resources will have tended to change in some way over time. You need to have a sense of not only what attributes have changed over time but also how they have changed for good or bad and what this can mean for you.

Again, this helps direct you to discover what has worked for you in the past and can still work for you in the present. It helps you see the new attributes you have discovered and how well they currently work for you. While exploring what has worked, you likewise need to determine and explore what hasn't worked in the past ... and may still not be working for you in the present. It likely will present itself as a habit.

EXERCISE: *Assessing Your Strengths*

In each category below (number 1 through 15) you are to put down what strengths and attributes you have had in the (1) *past* and what you have in the (2) *present*. Put in sentence form some positive thing you did using that strength or attribute first in the *past*. "I ______" and then in the *present*. "I ______."

For example, under "Character Strength," you might list *honesty,* as Tasha did. Therefore, in her sentence about her *past* she wrote, "I received too much change from a cashier and gave it back." About her *present* she wrote, "I returned a man's wallet when he dropped it at the bank's teller window." You need to be descriptive, concrete, and specific.

It's important you go through the whole exercise in one sitting, initially putting down at least *one* item per question. At first, recalling these may be difficult because you have likely not given them much concentrated thought before. However, initially doing it in one session forces you to get into the flow quickly. It also allows you to discover more examples of your positive attributes more easily over time.

By continuing to add responses as quickly as possible, you will further allow yourself to see the positive resources you have as well as what changes have occurred over time. This shows you a new, positive dimension of yourself that has been submerged.

1. Character Strengths
2. Abilities
3. Talents
4. Skills
5. Values
6. Appearance Strengths
7. Useful Connections
8. Knowledge Areas
9. Educational Strengths

10. Social Strengths
11. Thinking Strengths
12. Emotional Strengths
13. Physical Strengths
14. Spiritual Strengths
15. Family Strengths.

After you feel you have finished with your responses for each category, you need to go back to each response in each category and RATE it as to *importance* or value to you. Rank 1 as *no value/importance to me now* and 10 as *most value/importance to me now*. You need to become aware of what you particularly value, and of what you are most proud, in your strengths and attributes.

This demonstrates that you are anything but inadequate in any circumstance. In fact, it points out that you could get more of the things you want by using the resources you already have. This is because you are building a good and solid sense of yourself and your strengths. Knowing your competencies and feeling confident about them is what you can use as a basis for launching a plan to go after and achieve any of the things you want.

Progress Report:
(Answer the following in detail)

1. How many strengths and attributes have you listed overall?
2. In what categories do most of your strengths and positive attributes fall?
3. What do you see as your greatest strength(s) and attribute(s)?
4. How can you use those strengths and attributes to become more confident?
5. Which of your strengths and attributes make you really feel proud of yourself?
6. Describe a situation in which you positively used that strength or attribute and the positive result it achieved.
7. Make sure you recorded everything in your Daily Log.
8. Be sure to have spent several *days* on this designated section.

EXERCISE - *Looking at Your Positives*

The following exercise will show you how to re-assess what you possess as a human and worker in a true and positive light.

On the following items, you will be assigning POSITIVE attributes about yourself in each of the following categories. You are to look at *all* the aspects of your life (work, personal, family, community) and answer in each aspect of your life, as noted in *1a.* below. Be as truthful with yourself as possible—that is, no modesty or humility—and no discounting and dismissing achievements of any kind.

No "Don't know" responses. *No* negative responses of any kind. They're not only not useful but also self-defeating. Because of your fear you already tend to emphasize the negative. So now you need to begin to reverse that and look for and apply the positive.

To be your most effective you need to spend at least several days thinking over your responses in order to bring your submerged positives to the surface. This may not be easy for you initially since this also isn't how you've been thinking.

Start with *one* response per question. Then, as you think about it more deeply over time, continue to add responses. You want to make a *game* of it—a challenge, like doing a puzzle—and respond to each question with as many answers as you can generate.

1a. What you do well (in your work, personal, family, and community life)?

1b. Where do you apply these attributes or strengths?

1c. How do you apply these attributes or strengths?

1d. Where else could you apply them that you aren't doing now?

1e. What positive strength or attributes that you use outside work could you transfer to inside work?

1f. When you apply these attributes and strengths, how do you feel?

1g. How often do you think of these as "successes" and praise yourself for them?

2a. What attracts others to you initially?

2b. What is there *generally* and *specifically* about you that others like?

2c. How do you know when people are responding positively to you?

2d. What do you *think* when others respond positively to you?

2e. What do you *feel* when others respond positively to you?

2f. What do you *do* when others respond positively to you?

2g. What are some of the best positive responses you have ever received?

3a. What topics or subjects have you learned about in some depth?

3b. What do you consider some of your areas of life expertise?

3c. What do you consider your most important area of life expertise?

3d. What do you consider some of your talents generally and specifically?

3e. What do you consider some of your areas of work expertise in general?

3f. What do you consider some of your areas of work expertise specifically?

3g. What do you consider your most important area of work expertise?

4. What positive life lessons have you learned?

5. What makes you a special and unique person? (You *cannot* disagree with this.)

Progress Report:
(Answer the following in detail)

1. In what category (personal, work, family, community) do you feel most positive about yourself—what you do, have done, and can do?
2. How often do you demonstrate the positive things you know you can do?
3. Where do you demonstrate most often the positive things you can do?
4. Describe the last positive thing you did.
5. What did you *think* and *feel* about it *before*, *during*, and *after* it?
6. Make sure you recorded your exercises and Progress Report answers in your Daily Log.
7. Be sure to have spent several *days* on this designated section of the Stepping Stones in order to have completely understood and embedded what you discovered in your brain.

STEPPING STONE I – WEEK #2

§ § §

Now you need to look at your boss, what she does poorly, what she does well, and what her strengths and positive attributes currently are. You will compare yourself to your boss on your strengths and attributes. Forget about the power and status differential. You are looking at intrinsic skills and abilities only.

Remember that power and status differential are merely assigned to and part of your boss's' position. Furthermore, you need to keep in mind that this power or status differential has no bearing on your valuable skills, abilities, talents, expertise, and experience. Comparing yourself with your boss (social comparison) is natural, normal, and expected as long as it doesn't get in your way of your doing what you need to do for your job and yourself.

Frank saw his recently-promoted boss as possessing essentially the same skills that he himself had. He found this annoying. But he could have taken it as a positive. That there was really little difference between his boss and himself except for the role his boss had. Objectively comparing himself to his boss was only one of the many comparisons he began to make to increase his awareness. He also began to compare himself with others in his culture, society, groups he valued, and with specific beliefs and attitudes he considered important.

The more objectively you can do it the better. You likewise want to see if you are similar or dissimilar to those you admire or dislike. You want to do it to determine what those similarities and dissimilarities are. You want to do it to see what you might do to make yourself more like "them" to achieve similar goals or, in some cases, less like "them."

Stefan saw himself as another great doctor-to-be, like Albert Schweitzer. When he saw Dr. Schweitzer objectively as not perfect but a flawed human being, he could feel he didn't have to be perfect to contribute to medicine too. He could choose what similarities he wanted to follow, such as Schweitzer's "reverence for life," and what dissimilarities he wanted to discard, such as Schweitzer's apparent patronizing of native Africans and bringing in whites to assist him, instead of teaching blacks to be skilled workers to assist him in his clinic. Allying himself with positive aspects of his hero, he associated himself with the perceived power, status, independence, reverence, motivation, and confidence of his role model.

As you can see, these social comparisons can be very useful. They can let you know what the social expectations are for certain roles you may already have or want to have. They also can tell you what others are doing to meet those role expectations.

Tasha wanted to emulate Steve Jobs' creativity. She found that this comparison helped her determine the role and goal she wanted at work. Furthermore, it also suggested ways she could prepare to achieve that goal and then start to do so.

One of the things you need to recognize and keep in mind is that everyone has individual strengths, abilities, talents, skills, experience, and expertise in some areas. You and your boss simply have *different statuses* because you have *different jobs*. Because of your *different* jobs you and your boss may achieve *different* things for *different* reasons under *different* circumstances. “Different” is not better or worse ... it’s just *different.*

Always remember: There is nothing inherently special about someone who has the label of “authority” or “high status.” This means when you compare yourself negatively with your boss and high-status others, you are really comparing apples and oranges. The only *real* difference is that they have the role with accompanying authority and you don’t.

As a result, you need to dissect and re-assess the label “authority.” You need to determine ways you can respond to it. This means looking behind the label, evaluating what’s there objectively, and then removing the power from the label.

Titles and roles of authority figures are just that: “titles” and “roles.” They are things *given* to certain people in order to accomplish certain tasks or who have accomplished certain tasks. You and your boss are just trying to accomplish particular business goals through slightly different paths.

One of the things you need to do with someone in authority or high status is to mentally *erase* that individual’s label: their job title, role, or financial, social, business, professional, or celebrity status, et al. That is, you need to see him as a *person* first and in a *particular role* second.

Of course, you would still respect his title or role. You would still adhere to the accompanying protocol for interacting with that role and person holding it. But, when you interact with him, you would need to concentrate on what you need to do to for your task and to productively interact with him ... AND *forget* his label. You are communicating *person to person*. Otherwise, his label can be a hurdle for you to have to constantly leap over. That is, you can't do what you need to do and what you are expected to do.

EXERCISE - *Assessing Your Boss's Strengths*

Assess your boss's current personal and work attributes and strengths from what you know of them.

1. Character Strengths
2. Abilities
3. Talents
4. Skills
5. Values

6. Appearance Strengths
7. Useful Connections
8. Knowledge Areas
9. Educational Strengths
10. Social Strengths
11. Thinking Strengths
12. Emotional Strengths
13. Physical Strengths
14. Spiritual Strengths
15. Family Strengths.

Next you need to compare your attributes and strengths with those of your boss. Use as much time as necessary to develop the list comparison.

After you finish, ask yourself

- What did you discover?
- In what ways are you similar?
- In what ways are you different?
- What does this tell you about your boss?
- What does this tell you about yourself?

Progress Report:
(Answer the following in detail)

1. Where are you and your boss similar in attributes and strengths?
2. Where are you and your boss different in attributes and strengths?
3. What emotional/judgmental labels did you apply previously to your boss?
4. How have your emotional/judgmental labels for your boss influenced your thinking about who your boss is?
5. How have your emotional/judgmental labels for your boss influenced your thinking about what your boss legitimately can do?
6. What more positive and productive labels can you substitute for your current labels for your boss?
7. How has thinking about labels for your boss influenced how you label yourself?
8. Make sure you recorded everything in your Daily Log.
9. Be sure to have spent several *days* on this designated section.

When you fear your boss or anyone in that role of authority, you simply cannot do your best. Frank, Tasha, and Stefan all tended to ruminate about interacting with their bosses and try to make themselves seem invisible whenever possible. If you worry about being evaluated and how you can survive, your thoughts and emotions are focused on not being adequate. Specifically, when you are distracted, your thoughts cannot be focused on your being a productive person or worker. Your will performance suffers.

After all, how could you concentrate on your doing your best when you constantly feel the need to:

1. Analyze everything that your boss says and does—everything that happens on the job
2. Spend your time fretting about what it all means for you now in your job
3. Negatively anticipate what it may mean for you in the future in your job.

Consequently, when you allow yourself to be anxiously distracted, it isn't long before you begin to feel hypersensitive about whatever your boss says and does to see if it is related to your value, effort, results, and position at work. You also become more concerned about what you can say to your boss about anything for fear of being misperceived, misunderstood, sounding anxious, stuttering, gasping for breath, losing words or thoughts, saying the wrong things, and becoming negatively evaluated as a result.

Negative thoughts and feelings are harmful to your emotional and work health. If you let them continue, they will lurk in the back of your mind, tainting your every work thought, action, and interaction. They will quickly sabotage you:

- Taking up your time
- Negatively affecting your mood
- Creating anger and hostility
- Lowering your output
- Interfering with your interpersonal skills and social effectiveness.

As a result, you will, in essence, make what you fear become a reality.

When you are in the presence of someone high status or in authority, you need to check out what thoughts are running through your head and how you feel as a result. If you feel fear, inadequacy, anger, and/or powerlessness, you need to disengage yourself, step back, and analyze the reality of those thoughts and feelings.

You need to ask yourself: Is there really something specific and concrete you can pinpoint about which to be concerned ... or is your feeling just more of your anxiety about authority figures? Whenever you feel fear, inadequacy, anger, or powerlessness at work, you need to ask yourself *why*?

- What is going on that is triggering these feelings?
- Why are you responding to the situations as you're doing?
- What does that tell you?

You need to keep track of these daily emotional instances in a small notebook you carry with you throughout the day then record them each evening in a section of your Daily Log in a section entitled, "Anxiety Instances."

EXERCISE - *Creating Your Anxiety Instances Section*

At the end of each day you will copy your notes about your anxiety thoughts, feelings, and behaviors into your "Anxiety Instances" section of your Daily Log. It will cover *all* the times you experienced any authority anxiety during the day.

You should note

1. What happened
2. What the circumstances were
3. What your thoughts were when it happened
   4. What your specific feelings were
4. How your body responded to your feelings of anxiety
5. What you did as a result.

This exercise is to make you more aware of your anxieties and to begin to look more objectively at them. You need to step outside your negative emotion to see what your thoughts were and where you need to do a "reappraisal" of the situation.

Making a reappraisal is acting like a scientist. You are stepping back to see more realistically in context *if* what you thought, felt, or believed to be true *really is true*. You do this by asking yourself the following questions based on your notations:

1. What is really going on here—what is the situation?
2. Why am I responding to this situation with these particular thoughts and emotions?
3. What evidence do I have that what I'm thinking and feeling really represents reality?
4. What am I doing to handle the situation?
5. Am I handling the situation in a satisfactory way?
6. How do I really want to handle the situation?
7. What result (goal) do I really want here as a result of my actions?
8. How useful are my current thoughts and emotions in dealing with the situation to get that result?
9. How might I respond differently in order to achieve that result?

Progress Report:
(Answer the following in detail)

1. What sorts of *thoughts* have you had about your boss this week?
2. What have you *felt* about your boss when you thought about him or her?
3. In what ways have you felt distracted from your work and doing your best because of your thoughts and feelings about authority figures?
4. Over the week what thinking and emotional differences have you noticed in what you have recorded in your log?
5. Make sure you recorded everything in your Daily Log.
6. Be sure to have spent several *days* on this designated section.

STEPPING STONE I – WEEK #3

§ § §

In order to alleviate your fear, you have to control the elements that contribute to it: those cognitive (thoughts), emotional (feeling), and physiological (body response) factors. The most basic of these components is your physiological response. When you experience fear, your heart races, you breathe more rapidly and shallowly, you may shake, stammer, feel dizzy, or be unable to speak, for example. While Frank sweated, Tasha began to breathe rapidly, and Stefan felt his tongue disconnect from his brain.

Before you can address your feelings and thoughts about your fear, you need to alter your body's reaction to it. You need to slow down your heart rate and correct your breathing. As long as you feel your heart racing and are exhaling too much carbon dioxide, you will be less able to feel and be relaxed in order to address anything. You can lower your heart rate and rebalance your oxygen and carbon dioxide levels through abdominal (diaphragmatic) breathing.

Abdominal breathing is designed to calm you before, during, and/or after an anxiety-provoking event. It does this both by distracting you from thinking about your body's panic symptoms and by re-balancing your oxygen and carbon dioxide levels. Shallow upper-lung breathing provides too much oxygen to your brain, making you feel dizzy, disoriented, and even more panicky.

EXERCISE: *Abdominal Breathing*

To learn to breathe abdominally, you need to sit in a chair in a quiet room. Place both feet flat on the floor with one hand on your abdomen and the other on your chest. Your hands on your stomach and chest areas help you determine if you are breathing abdominally or from your upper lungs.

To the count of five (5) you will slowly and gently pull in your abdomen (not tightly) as you exhale through your nose. As you do this, your chest should remain as still as possible. Using your hands, you can check where movement is occurring.

Hold this for three (3) counts (think "1-2-3"). Slowly release your belly muscles to the count of five (5) (not moving your chest) and take a small breath. Be sure *not* to fill up your lungs or breathe so hard that your chest moves. This sequence is one complete *diaphragmatic exhalation-inhalation set.*

You will continue breathing in this manner, counting "1-2-3" each time for ten (10) breaths. Once you have completed ten (10) breaths, you will take a moment to see how you feel.

Abdominal breathing has nothing to do with either deep breathing or shallow breathing. It has to do with your stomach muscles doing the pumping, not your chest muscles. When you use your upper chest muscles, you tend to take in small, shallow breaths only, which can lead to hyperventilation. When you use your abdominal muscles, you tend to take in fuller, slower breaths which are calming.

You will take in long, small gusts of air. But be careful not to breathe too deeply. If you become short of breath at first, stop, and take one large breath. Then you can resume the slow abdominal breathing. It's important to always begin your breathing exercise with an exhalation, not an inhalation.

You will do this exercise at least three (3) times a day. For this to become a *habit* for you—something you do automatically in the presence of something anxiety-provoking, when you think about it after the fact, or anticipate it recurring—you will need to practice for about three (3) weeks to a month.

Mindfulness is another way to reduce your stress, fear, and anxiety. It is a systematic form of meditation in which you purposely focus and concentrate your attention on the present, accepting it without judgment. In a mindful state you become relaxed but alert, aware of your perceptible mental states and processes, your emotions, physical sensations, thoughts, and images. You are like a dispassionate observer of nature—your nature—but *only* in the present, not in the past or future.

EXERCISE: *Mindful Meditation*

You need to sit quietly in a comfortable chair in a quiet location and focus on your breathing. Let it come naturally. As you breathe, you likewise focus on a word, or mantra, that you say silently to yourself. It can be any word, but something short, like "om" or "one" is better.

As thoughts come to mind, let them pass through without evaluation or judgment as you continue to focus on your mantra and breath. Your challenge is to not attach yourself to any specific thought, idea, feeling, or sensation or let yourself think about the past or future. You want to go with the flow in the present.

Body sensations will become obvious, such as tickling, itching, tingling, or muscle discomfort. Notice them without concern or judgment. As in Progressive Relaxation, focus on your body from head to foot, successively noticing how that individual body part feels: tight and cool with minimal blood flow or heavy and warm with relaxing blood flow.

Next you will focus your five senses. What sights, sounds, tastes, smells, and touch do you experience? Label each sense you detect and let it pass without judgment.

Feelings will present themselves. You should label each emotion but not experience that emotion. As a scientific observer, you will note it, accept it, and let it pass without judgment.

When you begin your mindfulness meditation, your mind will likely wander. You may become judgmental of the thoughts or your progress. This is natural and expected. Simply redirect your focus to standing back and observing those thoughts or feelings. No one does it perfectly at first so be kind to yourself and just start again. It will take practice. Like learning anything worthwhile, it takes time for you to accomplish it.

But as you learn to observe and experience without evaluation, you will begin to see which of your thinking and feeling habits produce negativity and what produce a sense of well-being. Continued practice means greater awareness of everything that happens every day, accepting it nonjudgmentally, and feeling less anxious and stressed. It can improve not only your overall feeling of well-being but also your positive interaction with others. Mindfulness meditation needs to become part of your daily routine.

Progress Report:
(Answer the following in detail)

1. What do you notice immediately after you do your abdominal breathing relaxation exercise?
2. What differences have you noticed in your anxiety/fear after you have applied your abdominal breathing?
3. What differences in other body responses have you noticed over the week as you've been doing this breathing and relaxation exercise?
4. Over the week what thinking and emotional differences have you noticed in what you have recorded in your log?
5. What have you noticed in your mindful awareness of your thoughts, feelings, senses, and sensations over the week?
6. When you're not being judgmental about those thoughts, feelings, senses, and sensations, how are you feeling overall?
7. Make sure you recorded everything in your Daily Log.
8. Be sure to have spent several days on this designated section.

To deal with alleviating fear of your boss you have to deal not only with your body's physical response but also with your thinking response to the fear. It is your thoughts that can direct what you believe, how you feel about it, and what you decide to do as a result.

In order for you to become confident, you have to reverse those automatic negative thoughts you have about your boss and her or his power. Because anxiety triggers irrational and negative thoughts, you have to address those specific thoughts. One way to start is to *dispute* them.

EXERCISE - *Disputation of Automatic Negative Thoughts*

Starting this week, before you go to bed, you are to review something *negative*—one event—that happened during that day. It can be either major or minor. For example, your boss seemed to be looking over your shoulder at your computer monitor as you worked or you didn't receive a piece of mail you were expecting. You need to recall any negative or anxious thoughts you actually had about the event.

When told to speak to a worker about an error, Frank thought, "I can't do this." When Tasha was asked why she had chosen a particular design, she thought, "They know I'm a fake." When a senior physician asked a question of his interns on rounds, Stefan thought, "I don't dare open my mouth because I'll somehow put my foot in it again."

When you recalled that something negative,

- What had you said to yourself when it happened?
- How did you feel emotionally when it happened?

Next you will write down in your Daily Log the event and your thoughts and feelings about it. Then using the following format, you will dispute those thoughts.

The format you will use is the ABCDE Disputation Format. Below is a fictitious example of how you should work to respond. Since you are unlikely to be already doing this on a regular basis, you need to know that it will take a little bit of time to get used to doing it. It takes time for it to become a habit. But once it does, you can think of it and immediately and quickly apply it any time you encounter one of "those" situations in a briefer form.

A(ctivating Event)—*what is the factual event that started your negative thoughts*: "When I received the evaluations for the psychology seminar I taught, one evaluation said, 'I was extremely disappointed in this course. The professor was thoroughly boring. I've seen livelier corpses. Maybe a corpse should teach this course instead. Whatever you do, don't take this class!'"

B(eliefs)—*what are your beliefs about the other person or situation:* "That little punk expects that if class isn't in Dolby surround-sound with glitzy multi-media, it's a bore. If you present thoughtful material, their eyes glaze over. They think they are so entitled to not have to think or even work a little."

C(onsequences)—*what did you feel emotionally and do as a result:* "I was absolutely furious and ranted about it for hours. Later that day I was still fuming about how arrogant and spoiled the student was."

D(isputation) of Belief—*what did you see objectively about the person or event when you stepped back from the emotion*: "That really was rude of the student. I can understand it if someone doesn't like the course, but there is no reason to be nasty. However, I need to remember that that was only one evaluation. Most of the other students seemed to think the course was okay. I didn't get as high ratings as I generally do, however.

"A few students pointed out that it would be easier for them to grasp the material if I used video, PowerPoint, or even overheads. They weren't asking for Industrial Light and Magic, just something to make the material a little more accessible and stimulating. Maybe I've gotten a little bit lazy. I used to go out of my way to make sure I engaged the students. I notice I don't enjoy teaching this course as much as I used to. I guess I'm letting that show. Maybe I should view that evaluation as a wake-up call and spend a little time refurbishing the material."

E(nergization—*how you feel after doing the disputation*: "I felt much less angry. Still annoyed by the way that one student expressed her/himself but I was able to keep it in perspective. I didn't like admitting I had gotten a little lazy but I was able to focus that energy on productively updating the course. In fact, I feel more re-connected to the material and am looking forward to revamping the course."

What you will find after practicing this disputation numerous times is that you do not need to be so descriptive. I went on at length because that's what we all tend to do at first. Over time it will become easier for you to see and dispute your thoughts so you will be able to get to the core of the negative thought and feeling more quickly. As it becomes a habit, you will see its reality much faster and more clearly.

Once you can do that, you can reduce what you need to write to describe the individual steps in your thinking and disputing process. Thus, while I have emphasized your being brief in general, you will need to be a bit *more expansive initially* as you work your way through the disputation process for yourself.

Progress Report:
(Answer the following in detail)

1. How many times this week have you had negative fear thoughts about your boss?
2. What specifically did you think at those times?
3. How did you *want* to act as a result of that feeling and those negative thoughts?
4. What did you actually do as a result of that feeling and those negative thoughts?
5. Describe one disputation briefly step-by-step you did this week and what it told you.
6. Over the week what thinking and emotional differences have you noticed in what you have recorded in your log?
7. Make sure you recorded everything in your Daily Log.
8. Be sure to have spent several *days* on this designated section of the Stepping Stones in order to have completely understood and embedded it in your brain.

STEPPING STONE I – SUMMARY

Stepping Stone I (Basic Stage) has begun addressing your fear of your boss, and other authority figures in the workplace, by starting the process of altering your perceptions of what authorities are, what they can do, and how you need to think about them. It has addressed your strengths, attributes, and resources. It has also addressed the physiological component of your fear/anxiety and started you thinking about your dysfunctional automatic negative thoughts and how to address and reverse them as well.

In Stepping Stone II you will continue to work on your irrational and dysfunctional thoughts about your boss and other authority figures. As you work on them, you will work on your resulting behaviors as well as replacing negative habits with positive habits.

STEPPING STONE II – WEEK #1

§ § §

Stepping Stone II is your Intermediate Level. In order to alleviate your fear of your boss, you need to deal with each anxiety-associated behavior and work to alleviate their fear-related element. You do that by taking each fear behavior, such as avoiding your boss, and breaking it down to its very small, step-by-step components. The components are the successive chain of the behaviors that precede that specific, resulting fear behavior.

Because avoiding your boss, for example, is *not* just one behavior but, instead, a series of small sequential behaviors, you have to deal with each tiny succeeding fear behavior that leads up to it. You will work on each behavior step until you feel comfortable doing it and then move on to the next upward behavior step in the series.

Specifically, you will break down your resulting fear behavior into its successive components and then create an ascending sequence (a hierarchy) of these behavior steps in it from least anxiety-provoking to most anxiety-provoking. Then you will work your way up the steps, first in your mind and then in real-life, exposing yourself to each and becoming comfortable with it before you move on.

EXERCISE – *Anxiety Hierarchy*

You need to create your own fear hierarchy. Using the form below, you will pick a behavior situation that makes you anxious. You will break it down into the steps leading up to it, starting with the least anxiety-provoking step.

Using ten (10) steps for each anxiety situation usually makes each step from the least anxious to the most anxious small enough that you can successfully overcome and achieve it in a short time and feel good about your accomplishment.

Important: You need to work on your fear hierarchy *first* in your *imagination.* As you approach Step 1, you need to apply your abdominal breathing so you can become more physically comfortable with the step. You picture doing that step as you breathe until the anxiety passes. Then you move on to the next step. Once again you do your breathing while picturing the step until the anxiety passes.

Because altering your breathing doesn't involve any specific thought which could be distracting, abdominal breathing will not interfere with your focusing on feeling and letting go of your fear. However, it's important to note that other relaxation exercises wherein you have to talk to yourself about your body becoming relaxed *will* interfere with your concentrating on your anxiety thoughts and working your way successfully up the anxiety hierarchy. They are specifically for concentrating on relaxing the body should *not* be employed when you are actually working on your anxiety behavior situation steps.

Once you have gone through each of the ten (10) individual steps comfortably, you need to go through all the steps together in sequence in your mind. Only when you have done that comfortably, do you then need to recreate all those behavior steps, from least anxiety-provoking to most, in the real world. Once again you will work on individual steps, as you breathe abdominally, then string the steps together in sequence.

With reality being as unpredictable as it is, you may need to create some behavior *simulations* because the step situation on which you're working is hard to find in real-life or you need more time with it than reality permits. You can't always locate and experience that precise step under normal circumstances in a real-life situation. In those instances, you need to come as close as you can by visualizing some of the missing elements as you work on the step.

You will use the following example as your model for constructing your own authority-figure anxiety hierarchy. As I already mentioned, you always start with the behavior farthest from your goal and work your way toward your desired behavior result. You need to use this exercise for every fear behavior you want to overcome.

Stefan's Anxiety Hierarchy

Most Anxiety-Provoking

10. Being questioned by physician and interns, responding confidently, and accepting the feedback
9. Being called on to give report—being the center of attention
8. Waiting for the physician to ask for the report
7. Entering the patient's room
6. Preparing for those questions
5. Thinking about what questions may be asked by senior physician
4. Preparing the report, making it complete and logical
3. Gathering patient's presenting complaint and the results of tests for the report
2. Finding out what is needed to be covered for the report
1. Thinking about giving a report on a patient at rounds

Least Anxiety-Provoking

Progress Report:
(Answer the following in detail)

1. What behavior did you choose to work on?
2. What 10 behavior steps did you create to work on your anxiety with authority figures?
3. How clearly could you see each step in your mind as you worked on it?
4. How helpful was doing abdominal breathing as you thought about each step?
5. What exactly did you do to practice each step in the workplace?
6. How helpful was doing abdominal breathing as you actually worked on each step?
7. Over the week what thinking and emotional differences have you noticed in what you have recorded in your log?
8. Make sure you recorded everything in your Daily Log.
9. Be sure to have spent several *days* on this designated section.

When you feel anxious about a situation, it is easy to discount and dismiss your having actually been successful in a similar situation, or in any situation for that matter. Instead, you tend to see only those things you feel you have done either wrong or inadequately. As a result, you need to track both your daily anxieties *and* successes.

You need to be aware of what you do correctly, adequately, and well. (And, yes, you *do* do things correctly, adequately, and well.) You need to recognize and acknowledge that you have been successful. You *do* achieve things. It doesn't matter how small or big each individual success may have been; you achieved it.

You need to start thinking in terms of what you do achieve on a daily basis in your personal life and at work. By tracking your anxieties and successes, you can see changes in the number of occurrences of both your anxieties and successes—with anxieties decreasing and successes increasing.

EXERCISE – *Success Instances*

You will create a section in your Daily Log for your *Success Instances*. You will note during the day in your small notebook when you experienced any *success* (things you were doing that went right for you). Then at the end of the day, you will record all those success in your Daily Log. Specifically, you will note

- What happened
- What the circumstances were at the time
- What you thought when it happened
- What you felt emotionally when it happened
  What you felt physically when it happened
- What you did as a result.

A "success" can be anything that is positive for you that you helped create, like finishing a report on time or saying "Hello," to your boss. Frank managed to take a worker aside to speak with him. That was his biggest success that day.

You need to tell yourself

- How you helped create the success
- What a good thing it was to do.

You also need to let yourself feel good about the success. You need to dismiss the notion that the "success" is really inconsequential or trivial, or that it really only happened by chance. You need to actively take credit for it because your mind will tend to want to continue to discount your successes. Tasha tended to see her achievements primarily as a matter of being in the right place at the right time—in other words, "pure luck"—until her boss gave her an enthusiastic thumbs up on her latest proposal.

This means you will have to purposely acknowledge your daily achievements and dispute those thoughts that your success wasn't *really* a "success." Those negative thoughts and feelings about what you do right have become a habit over the years that you have to strive to reverse.

Your *Success Instances* section is to make you more aware of your many large and small successes in the present. Over time you will be able to chart the decrease in your anxiety and increase in your successes. Part of this will result from your increasing awareness of what you are thinking, feeling, and doing. Part will be from your using skills that lessen anxiety and increase confidence. And part will be your becoming actively, repeatedly, and positively involved in things you never thought you would do.

Progress Report: (Answer the following in detail)

1. What personal anxieties are you recording in your "Anxiety Instances" section?
2. What personal successes are you recording in your "Success Instances" section?
3. What work successes you are recording?
4. Which of these anxiety behaviors can you work on in your Anxiety Hierarchy?
5. Which of these successes would be good candidates for you to re-experience?
6. What would make this a particularly good success candidate for you to re-experience?
7. How might you use this success recollection in dealing with your fear of authority figures?
8. Over the week what thinking and emotional differences have you noticed in what you have recorded in your log?
9. Make sure you recorded everything in your Daily Log.
10. Be sure to have spent several *days* on this designated section.
11. You will find out how to create, develop, and use *Past Success Instances* in the next section.

STEPPING STONE II – WEEK #2

§ § §

As you just learned, because you are doing many things successfully, you need to remind yourself of them. But that is not all. You likewise need to remind yourself of your successes in the past. Specifically, you need to recognize and acknowledge that instances of things in the past that went well were indeed successes. You need to recognize and acknowledge that you have achieved and accomplished many of the things you set out to do, no matter how small or big.

You need to recall these past success instances so you can provide your brain with hard evidence that you are not inadequate—that you really, truly have been successful and that those successes matter. It's hard to dispute empirical data that show that, in fact, you currently do things right and have likewise have done things right in the past.

Keep in mind that your brain has no reason to simply accept general positive affirmations that you have been successful. Like saying, "I've been successful, I've been successful." Sorry. That just won't do it. To make your brain accept any past success you have to recall the specific success instance in all its sensory detail.

Frank recalled when he was in the 4th grade, "I gave a 4-minute speech on the Arabian horse, talking about the color of their skin, height at the withers, advantages of the breed, and how the horse was used. My classmates clapped and the teacher smiled when I finished. I felt great."

After you recall your past success instance, you need to record it in your Daily Log and then re-live it in your mind. This hard evidence helps you dispute your negative automatic thoughts about your not having had successes. This starts implanting the seeds of confidence. It gets you to see that you do indeed have a power that has been submerged. The more past success recollections you can create, the greater the reservoir of data you will have to dispute your dismissive thoughts about your accomplishments.

EXERCISE – *Past Success Recollections*

Applying your abdominal breathing, relax yourself in a chair in a quiet place, close your eyes, and let your mind drift to times, events, accomplishments in the past—from childhood on to adulthood. Think about times when you felt proud and good about yourself.

For example, when you rode your first two-wheeler; when you first took over a household chore that your mom, dad, or other adult usually did; when you were graduated from school; or when you had your first pet, cared for it seriously and lovingly, and it quickly grew to be your best friend. Tasha recalled the time when her grandmother cried when Tasha gave her a special picture frame for a picture of her deceased grandfather that had small photos of significant events in the couple's lives all around the perimeter of the frame.

As these instances come to mind, you need to concentrate on them and absorb the feelings and sensory information—the sights, smells, sounds, taste, and touch. You need to note:

- What went on—how the scene played out
- What you did
- How you did it
- What you thought at the time
- What you felt at the time
- How others responded to it
- How you felt as a result of their response to you.

You need to put yourself in the scene, be present, so you can fully re-experience and emotionally register every nuance of the event. You will re-create it, see it, and become emotionally involved in it. You are to do this daily. Then you will record this in detail in your Success Instances section of your Daily Log.

What this will do is build a repository of vivid, positive experiences you can recall when you feel anxious and doubt you can handle something. This will help build your self-confidence foundation. You can't believe you're a failure when you have a long list of concrete, specific successes at your fingertips.

Recalling and reliving successes is like the children's book, "The Little Engine That Could." The little engine started out thinking it couldn't pull the train over the mountain, saying, "I can't. I can't. I can't." But thinking about it more positively, it started saying, "I think I can. I think I can. I think I can." And when it acted and successfully pulled the train over the mountain, it finished by saying, "I thought I could. I thought I could. I thought I could." This is where your self-confidence comes from.

Once you have created your repository of general life success experiences, you then need to focus on your success experiences at *work*, specifically your interactions with your boss and other authority figures and create further at-the-ready success instances.

Progress Report:
(Answer the following in detail)

1. What success did you decide to re-live in all its positive detail?
2. How did you feel when you re-lived this success in your mind?
3. Describe some of the sensory details that make this recollection come alive for you
4. How do you feel when you repeatedly bring this success to mind?
5. Over the week, what thinking and emotional differences have you noticed in what you have recorded in your log?
6. Make sure you recorded everything in your Daily Log.
7. Be sure to have spent several *days* on this designated section.

A variation on the Disputation of Automatic Negative Thoughts is the Vulture and Coach. The pessimistic, automatic negative thoughts which constantly clang in your head come from your Vulture. The Vulture represents a selective, negative filter which allows nothing good to be said about you or by you to yourself.

The Vulture is how you think and believe about yourself as well as about outside events. It is perched on your left shoulder where it constantly whispers negative emotional things in your ear, such as "You're a failure. You're inadequate." Your goal is to out-reason and out-support the Vulture.

On your right shoulder is your Coach. Your Coach represents rational thought—reality—and counters all the Vulture's soul-destroying negative thoughts. It will dispute the Vulture's irrationality by countering it with facts and hard evidence to the contrary.

Acting in the shoes of your Coach, you will vigorously dispute those negative and pessimistic thoughts. When your Vulture starts spouting its irrational venom, your Coach will jump in to debate the Vulture. Your Coach keeps positively countering everything the negative Vulture says until the Vulture has nothing more to say. Your

Coach will always have more positives than your Vulture has negatives.

The Vulture has been whispering in your ear for as long as you have been feeling your fear. This means the Vulture currently has more power than does your Coach. However, when you take your Coach's position and dispute what the Vulture says, you can simultaneously over time grow your Coach and shrink your Vulture.

When something makes you feel self-conscious or panicky at work, the Vulture starts in immediately producing Anxiety Thoughts. You think, "I can't do this." The moment you detect an anxiety thought or negativity you will have your Coach counter it and state objectively that you can do it and why you can do it, giving a concrete example: Tasha's Coach said, "I *can* speak to my boss. *I have done it before* ... in the design meeting where I suggested we get our detailed meeting agenda ahead of time so we can prepare and everyone responded positively to my suggestion, even my boss."

Your Coach also addresses the rationality of what the Vulture says. If the Vulture says, "Your boss doesn't respect you." Your Coach says to the Vulture, "What specific and concrete evidence do you have that that is so? What other explanations actually make more sense under the circumstances?"

After your Vulture has whispered, "You can't do this!" your Coach challenges it, asking you, "What is there about saying a few words to your boss that makes you uncomfortable?" This approach helps get you to the crux of the negative thought.

This disputation process between the Vulture and your Coach continues until your Coach demonstrates the Vulture has no realistic or reasonable arguments for the negative self-conscious thoughts with which it pummels you.

EXERCISE - *Vulture and the Coach*

Choose an authority-figure-related event about which you feel negative, pessimistic, or anxious. If when you do the exercise you cannot remember the specific pessimistic, negative, or anxious thought about the event you have in mind, you can make up one that seems appropriate to the situation. Either way, the object is to counter the Vulture and dispute vigorously what it says. You can make a game of it, one you know you're going to win.

1. Write down the chosen situation. Next begin by writing down the first fear-thought (Vulture) you had about the situation.
2. Then, acting as an objective observer (Coach), respond realistically and rationally to that thought. Write down your objective response.
3. Now go back to the original fear-thought and analyze it: Ask yourself:
   - What is the basis of the problem for me?
   - What are the assumptions, attitudes, expectations, rules, or beliefs on which this thought is based?
4. Repeat this fear-thought assessment for other fear-thoughts that arise during this sequence.
5. Go over your rational responses to your fear-thoughts. This reinforces your successful rational thinking approach to what your Vulture says.
6. Do this exercise any time your Vulture whispers in your ear.

Use the following format:

Vulture (Negative Thought)

Coach (Realistic Assessment)

Origin of Negative Thought: What is there about ____ that makes me anxious/self-conscious?

Vulture (Negative Thought)

Coach (Realistic Assessment)

Origin of Negative Thought: What is there about ____ that makes me anxious/self-conscious?

Vulture (Negative Thought)

Coach (Realistic Assessment)

Origin of Negative Thought: What is there about ____ that makes me anxious/self-conscious?

As you dispute your Vulture, your Vulture runs out of steam because it can no longer successfully counter what your Coach says. Over time, the Vulture which has been towering over you gets smaller and smaller. Your Coach, on the other hand, gets bigger and stronger. Continuously repeating this exercise can cause your Vulture to disappear.

Progress Report:
(Answer the following in detail)

1. What does your Vulture constantly say to you?
2. What does your Coach say to respond to these particular negative statements?
3. What specific and concrete evidence does your Coach use to counter your Vulture?
4. What do you *think* when your Coach responds to your Vulture?
5. How do you *feel* when your Coach responds to your Vulture?
6. Over the week what thinking and emotional differences have you noticed in what you have recorded in your log?
7. Make sure you recorded everything in your Daily Log.
8. Be sure to have spent several *day*s on this designated section.

STEPPING STONE II – WEEK #3

§ § §

If given the choice of interpreting what you see and hear as positive or negative, when you have anxiety issues you will tend to spin it negatively. This is because you have to keep yourself vigilant of potential dangers in order to protect yourself. Anxiety makes survival foremost in your mind.

When you can step outside your current mindset, you can see that despite your current fear and negative thoughts, you are really a responsible, conscientious, productive professional. You can see that you actually do have power but it is simply a different form of power from that of your boss. You no longer have to stay vigilant. You no longer have to protect yourself.

Based on your past and present successes, your expertise, and experience, you no longer have to worry about your survival *unless* there is a concrete, specific cause to do so. Beliefs and feelings are not data. They are not concrete and specific data or a cause to worry about your survival.

Because you have been less likely to express yourself as you would have liked to your boss you now need to begin to experience doing so a little at a time, in an incremental process. But that is not all. Speaking to your boss and effectively expressing yourself requires more than just practicing your speaking to her or him. That is, you need to be aware of your boss's perspective on whatever the subject is. You need to communicate in a way that is clear, logical, focused, on target, and from your boss's (not your) point of view.

Because of your fear, you have tended to be concerned in most cases only about yourself. That is, you have been concerned primarily about what your perspective is, what you want to say, what you want to accomplish, and how you can get it over before your anxiety kicks in or something "terrible" happens.

To make any communication effective, irrespective with whom, you need first and foremost to listen. Listening requires that you step back, disengage from your emotion, and focus on the other person—what he or she says and means.

Listening is doubly positive. When you are focused on something other than your anxiety, you cannot feel anxious. That is, you cannot attend to two tasks or emotions at the very same time. Listening also helps you develop a sense of the other person's point of view which is necessary for real communication. The following exercise will help you further get to know your boss as a person, and not just a label or role or an object to fear.

EXERCISE - *Empty Chair*

In the Empty Chair Exercise you put two chairs facing one another. You sit in one chair and speak to the other chair as if it were your boss (you can also do this for any authority figure, issue, situation, problem, thought, emotion, or another person). You tell your boss what you *think* about some behavior, issue, or situation. You tell her or him how you *feel* about it. You tell him or her what you *want done* as a result.

You then change chairs and assume the chair/role of your boss and respond to what you said to her. This means you have to step outside yourself to assume your boss's persona and speak for her as you think she would respond.

- How do you think she would respond?
- What do you think she would say?

You then change chairs again and respond as yourself to your boss's responses. This should go on until you have expressed what you wanted to say and also have a better sense of your boss's beliefs, attitudes, intentions, and motivations. The object of this role play is two-fold. First, it is to get you comfortable speaking *aloud* to your boss about some issue. Second, it is to gain perspective by getting inside what you perceive to be your boss's different thoughts and feelings.

However, since this technique may initially seem anxiety-provoking for some, it may be useful for you to start by working with *neutral* topics. Then you can move to more emotional and anxiety-provoking ones. This will allow you to get the technique under your belt without adding more anxiety to an already anxiety-ridden situation. With that in mind, you are to start with example #1 and work your way through to #3.

1. Start with some movie you've seen either recently or in the past about which you had some criticism.

- Talk to the movie
- Tell it what you didn't like about it
- Tell it why you didn't like it.

Then you become The Movie and respond from the perspective of the movie— why it did what it did.

You again respond to what the movie says ... then have it further respond to you. See how far you can go so that you can listen and see both perspectives of the issue. (You can do this with a book or TV show as well.)

2. A spokesperson for the U.S.A. Tobacco Institute is calling for smoking in hospital patient rooms. Tell the spokesperson why you disagree with that stance. Lay out your arguments. Then have the spokesperson respond with their side—their arguments. Continue this debate until both sides have been aired and you have a better sense of all the arguments from both sides and their different perspectives.

3. Your friend has damaged your car slightly. Tell him how you feel about this. Have him respond as to how it happened, how he feels about it, and what he wants to do as a result. Continue until you have a sense of his side of it as well as your own *feelings*, not just thoughts, on the issue, and have expressed them.

Once you have successfully worked on the neutral examples of the Empty Chair Exercise above, you need to do the Empty Chair with your thoughts and feelings about your negative comparison to your boss's authority and your resulting pain/fear. Then have your boss tell you

- What her valuable attributes are
- Why those particular attributes are "superior" to yours for the role of "boss"
- Why she as a person is more worthwhile than you in the workplace
- Why she has the authority and you don't.

Then you are to address the "superiority question"—that is,

- Why she doesn't objectively really know more in a particular area than you do
- Why she doesn't have more or better skills, abilities, expertise, experience than you do
- What differences do exist in your respective workplace roles and activities
- Why those differences don't have anything to do with superiority.

You want this interaction to stay civil, assertive, but respectful. This means you don't want to let yourself get angry or aggressive in what you say or how you say it. In response to what an authority figure says about his strengths, you should *praise him* for what he has. You then can *add what your strengths are*, based on your attributions and strengths' assessment, in that area as well. This is *not* one-upmanship. It is only sharing (and practicing sharing) that you have strengths as well.

You have your boss reply as you think she would if she really were to express her "superiority." You want to employ examples of your strengths and her results. You will continue talking to the Empty Chair until "your boss" has little to say and you have expressed yourself fully on the topic.

While this discussion is not one you and your boss are ever likely to have, this exercise gives you practice talking to the authority figure on an emotional issue. It has you standing up for yourself assertively and calmly, expressing and defending your strengths, attributes, and value, thereby reinforcing that you are worthwhile as a person and employee. You can see your boss as a real person on equal footing with you, as human and not a symbol of superiority.

It also helps you see the authority figure's likely perspective. Of course, you can't know exactly what your boss's intentions, motivations, perspective, and thinking are in general or at any given moment. You can only infer these things from his role, the body language you observe, his behaviors, what he says, and how he says it.

Once you have the technique down, you can do away with the physical chairs and switch roles in your mind. However, speaking the roles *aloud* is essential. It provides sensory reinforcement of what you say and how confident you feel and sound doing it. You need to do this exercise at least three (3) times a week.

Thereafter, any time you have a problem with your boss, another authority figure, or anyone else for that matter, doing an Empty Chair dialogue can help you see both your perspective and the possible perspective of the other person. This can go a long way in helping you feel in control and expressing yourself within that control. It can both address the real issues and keep emotion-based assumptions about the other's intentions to a minimum. This allows you to listen so you can focus on the core issue at hand.

Progress Report:
(Answer the following in detail)

1. What did you say to your boss during the Empty Chair?
2. How did you say it?
3. How did you feel as you did it?
4. How did your boss respond to it?
5. What did you think about what your boss said?
6. How did you feel about it?
7. What did you think about your boss as a result of the interaction?
8. What did you learn about your boss's perspective?
9. In what ways did your own perspective about your boss change as a result?
10. Over the week what thinking and emotional differences have you noticed in what you have recorded in your log?
11. Make sure you recorded everything in your Daily Log.
12. Be sure to have spent several *days* on this designated section.

One technique that is very useful to help you remain calm is *Distraction*. In other words, you can interrupt the neural pathway that creates your experience of fear of authority figures—or any social fear or anxiety—by using simple, easy-to-employ thought disruption techniques.

For you to feel your fear, you have to go through the sequence that makes up your habitual fear pattern. When you interrupt that sequence, you cannot maintain that same level of fear during and after the disruption. When you disrupt the sequence permanently, you can help eliminate your fear habit.

It is important to note, however, that these strategies are for the *temporary* reduction of anxiety symptoms. That is, they are *not* for total elimination of the whole of fear of authority figures, social anxiety, or any other anxiety disorder. For that you have the basic cognitive-behavioral strategies which are employed throughout this program. Distraction, then, in its many forms, is simply an additional technique to employ when you don't feel you have time to do a full breathing exercise, for example.

EXERCISE - *Using Distraction*

Distraction is employing mechanical and other means to interrupt your fear or negative emotion. There is a long list of techniques which you'll need to try in different anxiety-provoking situations to see how they work for you. Knowing about them all gives you a choice when you need a distraction in a hurry and don't want to have to search your mind for one or try to make up one. Having to spend time dredging up something will only add to your anxiety. This means you need to practice all of the following to see which ones are best tailored to you.

1. Putting up a physical, or mental, hand and saying, "Stop!"

2. Pinching yourself hard on the arm

3. Dropping something

4. Coughing three (3) times

5. Squeezing your toes four (4) times

6. Whistling a popular tune

7. Humming your favorite melody

8. Retying your shoe laces

9. Poking a friend in the ribs

10. Reciting the lines of a poem, song, or prayer
11. Snapping an elastic band on your wrist
12. Playing with objects in your pocket
13. Counting backward from 20 to 1 by threes
14. Clicking a ballpoint pen
15. Cleaning your glasses
16. Drinking something
17. Putting a piece of gum, candy, or breath mint in your mouth
18. Blowing your nose
19. Writing your name backward on a piece of paper
20. Using a mirror to check to see if you have food on your teeth
21. Clicking a clicker in your pocket three (3) times
22. Rolling a quarter across your fingers
23. Counting from 1-10 in another language
24. Recalling seven (7) first names of females beginning with the letter "D."

Progress Report:
(Answer the following in detail)

1. Which distraction methods did you try?
2. Which methods worked particularly well for you?
3. In what situations did you find they worked best?
4. What other methods you've found that worked could you add to this list?
5. Over the week what thinking and emotional differences have you noticed in what you have recorded in your log?
6. Make sure you recorded everything in your Daily Log.
7. Be sure to have spent several *days* on this designated section.

STEPPING STONE II – SUMMARY

Stepping Stone II has concentrated on your working on your negative thinking habits and reversing them. These thinking habits are one of the primary causes of your fear and anxiety about interacting with authority figures. To deal with them you have to break down your negative thoughts into behavioral steps then address each one by itself. When you are working with small parts of a larger task, it is easier to accomplish the larger task. You achieve one step successfully then go to the next. The overall result is that you feel more and more confident about your ability to accomplish these tasks and continue these achievements.

You have worked on numerous ways to change negative thoughts into positive thoughts. The core of most of these techniques is questioning, analyzing, and debating your negative thoughts to see to what degree they represent *reality* and countering them with reality when they don't.

Other techniques provide quick ways to quickly interrupt anxiety so you can stand back to more objectively observe your thoughts and their accompanying emotional reaction. When you take yourself out of the negative thought–negative emotion feedback loop, you keep yourself from being caught up in escalating negativity and fear.

Stepping Stone III will expand on some previous techniques and provide others that you can find useful in coping with your anxiety and increasing your confidence. You will see how to reward yourself for all the positive things you do. Moreover, you will discover how to communicate effectively with authority figures, including your boss.

The more ways you have to see that you have been successful, are currently successful, and can be successful in the future, the more flexibility you will have in dealing comfortably with alleviating your fear and interacting with your boss in the best way for you.

STEPPING STONE III – WEEK #1

§ § §

As you are making progress in your thoughts, feelings, beliefs, and behaviors, it is essential that you *reward* yourself in a more formal fashion. You are making significant progress in positively changing your thoughts, feelings, and behaviors and your progress demands to be rewarded. Now instead of just feeling good about a successful situation, you will deliberately demonstrate that you acknowledge and accept that what you have achieved represents a *success—your* success. And each and every one of your successes deserves—and must receive—praise and a reward!

EXERCISE - *Praise and Reward List*

To demonstrate your acknowledgement and acceptance of your successes, you need to create a reward ritual. Specifically, every time you achieve something, no matter how small or large, you need to *physically* pat yourself on the back. This is important.

At the same time, you need to say aloud (even if you have to whisper it to yourself), *"That was a success. I am proud of myself for doing that. I knew I could do it. Everyday I'm seeing more of my successes. Everyday I'm getting more and more successful. This feels really good."*

Then you need to make up a list of graded rewards from which you can choose to reward each success. You need to continually add new items—both tangible and intangible—as you think of them. The more you have the better.

Rewarding yourself is like giving a dog a puppy biscuit to reinforce its having done something positive. What this does is show yourself that you *know, believe,* and *accept* that you deserve to feel good about your accomplishments. It lays another brick in your self-confidence foundation.

At first you may feel this is silly, patting yourself on the back and saying the praise phrase. Or, you may reject that you have done anything that really merits a reward. Even if you feel that way, you need to go through the praise-reward behavior ritual. Even if you do not as yet feel what you do is a "success" or deserves a reward, you need to do it because merely doing the sequence of behaviors in the ritual will start the reinforcement of your awareness of your having achieved successes. Awareness always precedes change in thoughts, feelings, and behaviors. Awareness plus positive reinforcement create positive habits.

For far too long you have discounted and dismissed your successes. Now your overriding thought needs to be, "Forget humility. I've done something important. I know it. I feel it. And I *deserve* to be rewarded for it!"

Rewards can be anything that you like. The List can run from something as small as a few-minutes' break or a candy bar or piece of gum or reading a few pages from your current novel to something larger, like going out to dinner or buying yourself something you have wanted. Make sure you create a section in your Daily Log entitled *Praise and Rewards*.

You should have as many rewards as possible from which to choose. But while it's easier to think of tangible rewards, like a Starbucks Mocha Frappuccino, rewards should not all be tangible. They can include meditating for a few minutes, watching the birds flying around, taking a walk, enjoying the setting sun over the trees, or humming a favorite tune. You're the one who decides what type of reward fits what specific success.

As I said, the reward you choose for each and every success should be commensurate with the level of the success. A small success means a small reward. A large success means a large reward. But, no matter what, you *have* to reward each and every success. Nothing positive you accomplish is too "trivial" to be praised and rewarded.

With respect to creating your Reward List, if you have any problems with procrastination, you might want to include in your List those activities you have found to be "time wasters" when you need to concentrate on a specific task. This means you can use those "time wasters" to reward yourself as long as you scope the amount of time you allow for yourself to do them.

Using "time wasters," like playing solitaire, playing a cyber-game, or checking out YouTube videos or desired products on eBay as rewards keeps you from feeling deprived of what you really like to do (and tend to do when you don't want to do what you *need* to do). It shows you can do what is necessary and *still* do what you'd rather do. It gives you a sense of control over your time. That is, you control it rather than it controls you, as is often the case in procrastination and inadequate time management.

Be sure to record each success you praise and reward. Your Reward List also needs to be in your *Praise and Reward* section where you can add to it and refer to it often.

Progress Report:
(Answer the following in detail)

1. What kinds of graded items have you added to your Reward List?
2. To what degree do they reflect both tangible and intangible rewards?
3. How often did you acknowledge your success with a back pat?
4. How often did you acknowledge your success with praise?
5. How often did you acknowledge your success with a reward?
6. What has been the hardest thing to do regarding praising and rewarding yourself?
7. How has your acceptance of your rewarding successes changed over the week?
8. Over the week what thinking and emotional differences have you noticed in what you have recorded in your log?
9. Make sure you recorded everything in your Daily Log.
10. Be sure to have spent several *days* on this designated section.

If you find that anxiety-interruption techniques work well for you in those moments of needed distraction, you may want to try these other techniques as well and add them to your bag of fear-reducing tools. The more you have to work with the more effectively and efficiently you can calm yourself when there isn't time for a full session of abdominal breathing. That doesn't mean, however, that you shouldn't try to apply your abdominal breathing anyway. You should for as long as is necessary. But *combining the two can relax you even faster!*

EXERCISE - *Other Ways to Interrupt Anxiety*

1. Think about a positive, emotionally-loaded subject that has meaning for you. Don't just think about it in the abstract, but *visualize* it in detail and feel it with all your senses. For example, think of your mother or father or other individual showing you affection. Think about watching a gorgeous sunset shared with a close friend, getting a job you wanted, getting a fantastic deal on audio equipment, or finding out someone that you liked also liked you.

2. Picture yourself in a warm shower. You can feel the enveloping warmth. Each of the little needles of water is stabbing your skin on your neck, shoulders, and back, stimulating them. Visualize your white, tense, knotted shoulder and neck muscles slowly beginning to unknot. As your muscles untie themselves, they become longer and looser. They are like loose, wide rubber bands. Oxygenating blood is filling them. Now they are becoming redder, warmer, and heavier. As your neck, shoulder, and back succumb to the gentle beating massage, you feel more and more relaxed.

3. Substitute a competing emotion for your fear. Conjure up humor by telling yourself the silliest, dumbest, or funniest joke you've ever heard. Or conjure up sadness by grieving over your grandfather's or a pet's death. You cannot think of and experience two competing emotions at once. If it is proactive, the emotion you are introducing will tend to be disruptive of your fear and take precedence over it.

Whenever possible, make the substituted emotion an upbeat, positive one, like happiness, humor, or excitement. This is because it is an activating emotion that focuses your attention outward. Only in situations where you cannot manage to conjure up a positive emotion should you use a more negative one, such as sadness. This is because negative emotions tend to focus your attention inward, which is where you are already focused when you feel any social fear or fear of authority figures.

Anger can be directed either inwardly or outwardly. While it is a very activating emotion, it should be used very *cautiously* because it can reinforce the negativity you already have and are trying to eliminate. Many people who have social fears, such as fear of authority figures, also feel a lot of anger because of its frustration. Therefore, anger should be the emotional substitute of last resort.

4. EMDR (eye-movement desensitization and reprocessing, which may use eye movement, dichotic hearing, and alternate finger tapping) has been shown to help some people alleviate their trauma and anxiety. While controversial, some limited research has indicated its results to be on par with cognitive-behavioral therapy in dealing specifically with Post-Traumatic Stress Disorder. The reason for this is considered unclear.

A. You should sit comfortably in a quiet environment. Do your abdominal breathing to settle and calm yourself. Decide ahead of time what method you will use: eye movement, shifting hearing, or tapping. For eye movement have two lights in front of you about three feet apart. For alternate hearing record clicks such that one goes to the right ear then to the left using head phones. For tapping determine what you will alternately tap (other hand, leg, or chair).

B. As you think about an anxiety-provoking situation with a past authority figure, you will execute your method (repeatedly moving your eyes from right to left while keeping your head still, listening to the right then left clicks, or tapping right then left).

C. As you think of the anxiety-provoking event, you are to repeat the following aloud to yourself for five (5) minutes:

- "I feel safe and calm."
- "I am strong and resilient in mind and body."
- "I am at ease with myself."
- "I am confident in what I say and do."

You need to memorize these four assertions.

Progress Report: (Answer the following in detail)

1. What positive, emotionally-loaded subject did you think about?
2. How did it affect your feelings of anxiety?
3. Describe how the visualized shower made you feel.
4. Describe how you could do something similar with taking a tub. What would that experience be like?
5. How did the shower and/or tub affect your anxiety?
6. What competing emotion did you conjure up?
7. What effect did it have?
8. How did the EMDR affect your anxiety and fear?
9. What techniques did you find worked better for you?
10. Over the week what thinking and emotional differences have you noticed in what you have recorded in your log?
11. Make sure you recorded everything in your Daily Log.
12. Be sure to have spent several *days* on this designated section.

STEPPING STONE III – WEEK #2

§ § §

As I've mentioned before, re-experiencing your recalled Success Instances is an effective way to present specific and concrete evidence to your brain and negative belief system that you have been successful. It reminds you of what you did and how it felt. This is useful any time you need a confidence boost.

To help make your recalled Success Instance even stronger and more effective you need to create a Walt Disney nature film of it in your head. That is, you need to create a sensory-loaded visualization you can play over and over. It should be scripted and have a beginning, middle, and end. The more detailed you make it as a mental film, the more impact it will have. And the more quickly it will enhance your self-confidence, self-esteem, and sense of control as well as put you in a more positive mood.

Your providing a narrative—pinpointing what you're seeing, hearing, feeling, smelling, tasting, and thinking—reinforces what you are seeing, hearing, feeling, smelling, tasting, and thinking. It further increases your recollection and enhances your in-depth experience and its effectiveness.

EXERCISE – *Visualization*

You will pick one of your earlier Success Instances. Building on your earlier recollection, you will recreate it as if you were going to create a full-blown movie of it. To do this you need to go back in time in your mind and actually

1. *Re-live* what you were doing step-by-step as it happened
2. Experience in detail how it felt to be doing it
3. Experience in detail what you saw, felt, heard, smelled, touched—bring it to life
4. Experience in detail all that was going on around you in the environment (where were you, what were you wearing, who else was around, what were they doing, etc.)
5. Experience in detail how you felt when you found you were being successful
6. Experience in detail how you felt afterward

7. Experience in detail what you did as a result (where you were, what you were wearing, who was around, what were they doing, etc.) 8. Narrate the video as you are seeing, thinking, hearing, smelling, touching, feeling, and doing the action.

You need to get into all your senses. Your need to see exactly how things happened and progressed. You need to remember what you thought and felt when you completed it, and how you felt and what you did when you saw it was a success.

You need to set aside 30 minutes twice a day to do this. During this time, you need to sit comfortably in a chair and let you mind wander back to the incident. You've already conjured up this Success Instance so now you will be significantly enhancing it.

The objective of this exercise is for you to create a mental video of that incident that is so splashy, emotional, action-oriented, or dramatic that you can easily and eagerly re-run it in your mind whenever you start to feel lacking in confidence. The more Success Instances you recreate as Steven Spielberg–George Lucas extravaganzas in your mind (doing them one by one, of course), the less able your mind will be to discount and dismiss your successes and your deserved recognition for them. Your confidence will increase by leaps and bounds the more you do this and the more effectively you do it. *Practice, practice, practice.*

Frank created a visualization of his agonizing, anxiety-ridden work with a coach preparing for the job interview which he ultimately aced and was rewarded with the supervisory position at the auto assembly plant.

Tasha created her visualization around her first computer design project—months in the making—which she almost didn't submit to a state-wide competition, sure it was inadequate, and won first prize, confirming that she was on the right career track.

Stefan created his visualization around saving the life of a man who had collapsed on the street, having an apparent heart attack, wherein Stefan dialed 911 and immediately started CPR, resuscitating the man as the ambulance arrived.

These visualizations provide hard, indisputable evidence that you have been successful in the past AND that you can be successful again in the present and future. The more you acknowledge your successes the more powerful you will feel ... and be, as a result.

Of course, you can use visualization for following a step-by-step plan you develop for accomplishing anything. It's the same process. You see yourself doing what you need to do, feeling confident, and finally accomplishing it. Athletes of all kinds use visualizations.

Runners for the Boston Marathon, for example, see themselves running the 26-mile 385-yard course. Starting in Hopkinton, they traverse Routes 135, 16, and 30 to meet and stride up Heartbreak Hill near Boston College. It's at this point, 20–to–21 miles into the race, that they are most likely to "hit the wall" as muscle glycogen stores are depleted. But they continue onto the Boston streets, feeling up, alert, and energized as they near their goal and cross the finish line.

Visualization is a form of practice and rehearsing. When you finished going through your Anxiety Hierarchy, you created a visualization of the complete process. You could see yourself moving from start to finish like running your own Boston Marathon.

Progress Report:
(Answer the following in detail)

1. What success instance did you script and work on?
2. How many of your senses did you employ in your recollection visualization (hearing, seeing, touching, smelling, tasting)?
3. What else can you do to make the visualization even more impactful and memorable?
4. How easily and quickly can you run and involve yourself in your mental movie?
5. In what general life situations have you used this technique?
6. In what work situations can you see yourself using this technique?
7. Over the week what thinking and emotional differences have you noticed in what you have recorded in your log?
8. Make sure you recorded everything in your Daily Log.
9. Be sure to have spent several *days* on this designated section.

In order for you to speak with your boss or other authority figure, you have to know that you have a right to do it. That is, you have the right to stand up for yourself and speak respectfully to others to express your opinions, share information, ask questions, to communicate whatever you need or want to. Because you happen to be in a lesser-power position (don't think "subordinate") does not mean you cannot interact with your boss as you want and need to.

Standing up for yourself is called *Assertiveness*. It is not aggressiveness which is not being respectful and infringing on another's rights in order to get what you want. It is not non-assertiveness either which is not being respectful to yourself, wherein you act submissively and do not do what you want and need to.

There are four assertiveness techniques that you can use to help you communicate better, more accurately, and more clearly. They can make your interactions more effective and efficient. They provide ways to respond comfortably. Moreover, they help you feel good about yourself for saying what you need to say and asking for what you want.

Created by Manuel J. Smith in *When I Say No I Feel Guilty,* these skills help you to be firm and stick to your firmness while being calm, pleasant, and respectful. They are basic scripted responses you can have available whenever you need them.

Having them with you all the time on the tip of your tongue means you do not need to re-create the wheel whenever a problem arises. Because they fit all types of situations, you don't have to conjure up something from scratch each time you encounter a difficult, conflict-ridden, or panicky situation.

When you have these four responses always available, you can know what to expect, know how to respond, and be prepared to handle it nearly any situation.

1. *Broken Record* is the calm repetition of what you want. It is brief and to the point. The technique teaches persistence in your achieving your goals. It reinforces your determination and allows you to ignore the other person's irrelevant logic, manipulation, baiting, or trying to influence you.

For example, when Frank was looking for a particular brand of canned tomato paste in the grocery store, the person stocking the shelves kept telling him, "You don't really want that one; it isn't very good." Frank responded with a positive statement instead of his usually socially-anxious, "Oh, okay." He stated calmly and pleasantly, "I want that tomato paste." For every argument the store employee posed, Frank simply repeated the phrase, “I want that tomato paste.

You would do the same, “I want XYZ” or “I'm looking specifically for XYZ.” Like Frank, you do it like a broken record until you got what you wanted. This allows you to be the one making the decision for yourself about whatever you are seeking, like the tomato paste, instead of letting the store employee, or anyone else, make it for you.

2. *Fogging* is calmly accepting the probability that there *may be* some kernel of truth to what the other person says about you or the topic of conversation. At the same time, it allows you to be the ultimate judge of what you want to do and what you do. This is what Frank did next. He said to the store employee, "I understand how you might feel that way, but ... " then he added the Broken Record phrase, “I want that tomato paste.”

The technique shows empathy with the other person. You are listening and hear them. Empathy is the ability to be sensitive to the thoughts and feelings of others and to treat them as you want to be treated. The technique allows you to receive any criticism or argument without becoming defensive or anxious.

Fogging phrases include "That may be true," "I understand that," and "I'm sure you believe that." These initial phrases acknowledge your hearing the other person and reflect what is being said. You follow it with "but" then add your Broken Record.

3. *Negative Assertion* is the calm acceptance of your own errors or failings by agreeing with the criticism, *at least in spirit*. That is, you look at the suggested negatives about you without becoming unduly anxious and defensive. You agree with the "accurate assessment" framework which will reduce the critic's hostility and anger. However, it is *you* who decides if the description is accurate, exaggerated, overly emotional, and/or negative.

For example, when Tasha under-estimated the time needed to finish a project and her boss became frustrated and angry because of high-level demands for the final report, her boss said, "You really screwed up. We may lose the account. Now my butt's in a sling."

Using Negative Assertion Tasha responded, "You're right. I really did under-estimate the time to finish the project." Notice that what she did was acknowledge the *kernel of truth* in her boss's statement *but* she did so within her *own* frame of reference.

Specifically, she did not buy into any of the boss's emotion, exaggeration, and bias. She made her own decision about how much of what he said was true. She was the one deciding how much of what he said may really have applied to her but she did it assertively, not aggressively, and on her own terms.

4. *Negative Inquiry* is prompting your critics to tell you more about what's bothering them. This allows your critics to become more assertive and express their honest negative feelings. It also allows you to seek out critical information more comfortably to open up communication channels.

When Stefan's young spouse said to him, "You spend all your time on work-related projects," he responded calmly and neutrally, "What is there about my spending a lot of time on work that bothers you?" Then his spouse admitted her frustration, "You're buried in patient files and books all the time." Next, he asked, again calmly and neutrally, "What is it about my spending so much time with patient reports and books that's bad?" Etc.

Each inquiry helped him peel the onion to get him closer to the underlying problem, which may have been several layers down. In this case, Stefan's wife was feeling ignored, taking second place to medicine. Negative Inquiry is determining what the other person is really trying to express. It is also determining what really needs to be addressed, not the layers above it which may be unrelated and take you off on tangents, leaving the problem remaining.

EXERCISE - *Becoming Assertive*

These four techniques need to be learned and practiced every day, three (3) times a day. You should start with #1 Broken Record and practice, practice, practice. Create situations in your mind wherein you ask for something and have to keep asking for it. Very often you don't get direct responses to what you want. You simply keep repeating pleasantly but firmly what you want.

Write out a scenario and script for yourself. This actually will come to feel like a game once you get into it. You begin by saying it in your mind in response to imagined conversations. Then once you feel comfortable saying it in your mind, you take your script on the road. You try it out in real life then keep looking for opportunities to use it.

Let me give you a personal example of how simple and universal the application process can be. When I moved to California, I discovered one box of classical albums was missing when the moving company unloaded my shipment. I made note of it, informed the movers, and then sent a letter to the moving company.

They called me, "Everything you moved was in one shipping case which was completely unloaded."

I responded, "That may well be so but the box numbered 354788 was not checked off as having arrived. Your movers and I have searched and found it's not here. I want my box of classical albums."

Several calls later as they tried to dismiss my claim, I was still repeating my Broken Record and Fogging. I was ready to do it as long as I had to because I knew what to say and actually enjoyed saying it to them. Finally, they gave in and paid my claim.

It is surprising to see how you'll have more *yeses* than the other person has *noes*, so to speak. This develops in you a sense of persistence, strength, power, and confidence in standing up for yourself.

After you have worked on your Broken Record, go onto #2 Fogging. You work on it in the same way—first in you mind then in real life. Remember it is just your expressing your understanding of what the other is saying with the addition of your repetition of what you want. As you work on Fogging three (3) times a day, you are also working on Broken Record.

You then work on #3 Negative Assertion and then #4 Negative Inquiry while continuing to practice #1 and #2. If you are like most people, you will find #4 a little difficult initially because it requires you to disengage from your emotion when someone appears to be criticizing you. But if you are to find out what is really behind what is being communicated, you cannot let yourself be emotionally bogged down in the "criticism" and/or a defensive response to it. You have to focus on the core, what is being said. Then you need to analytically find out what the other person really means and what it really means for you.

These techniques are so simple and yet so powerful. They give you a way to know what to expect and how to prepare for it. Knowing you have a prepared script to address situations gives you confidence. You aren't going to be left anxiously grasping for the right thing to say to get what you want. That helps you remain calm and in control.

Feeling in control, on top of things, is essential to self-confidence. You can easily and quickly find the words you need. Using Fogging with Broken Record is great for dealing with disagreements: "I'm sure you feel that way, but I don't (or I disagree)." It is you who chooses what to answer, what you will say, and how you will answer. That is your decision and yours alone.

Note: It's important that you *not* feel you have to answer any and all questions asked of you by anyone. Because of your fear you may feel compelled to answer any questions posed by authority figures. Questions that are *important and relevant* to what you do and your job are questions that likely require answers.

However, you do not have to answer personal questions. Your best response to a question that you don't want to answer is to smile and say, "I'd prefer not to answer that" or "I'd prefer not to share my personal life (or feelings on the subject)." Be pleasant and honest but indicate how you feel. If, however, you feel there may be a legitimate reason for asking, you can use Negative Inquiry: "What is there that makes you ask that question?" If, on the other hand the person just seems to be nosy and persists, you can pleasantly change the subject.

When you choose to answer, in order to be more assertive in your answers and in control of your part of a conversation:

- Immediately neutralize the emotion of what they've said and look for the basic question or statement. You don't want to get hung up on negative emotion which can distract and overshadow everything else. You need to step back to evaluate what's at the core of the question of statement.
- Don't automatically accept *their* interpretation of the situation or issue (they have their perspective, motives, intentions, and agendas; you have yours). Use your own interpretation.
- Redefine, or reframe, the situation or problem in your *own* terms, according to your own thinking. Make it as emotionally neutral and reasonable as possible.
- Don't automatically answer questions *as they are asked.*
  Respond in a way that communicates the essential information they are seeking and *only* what you wish to communicate. But you do so in a way that allows you to be the judge—the decision maker, the one in control—and not one on the defensive, feeling compelled to answer anything and everything that is asked of you.

Progress Report: (Answer the following in detail)

1. What scripts did you create to practice Broken Record?
2. Where did you use Broken Record in real life and what happened?
3. What scripts did you create for Fogging?
4. Where did you use Fogging in real life and what happened?
5. What scripts did you create for Negative Assertion?
6. Where did you use Negative Assertion in real life and what happened?
7. What scripts did you create for Negative Inquiry?
8. Where did you use Negative Inquiry and what happened?
9. Over the week what thinking and emotional differences have you noticed in what you have recorded in your log?
10. Make sure you recorded everything in your Daily Log.
11. Be sure to have spent several *days* on this designated section.

STEPPING STONE III – WEEK #3

§ § §

Before you speak to your boss or any authority figure it's important for you to know that your *best responses* will depend upon the situation. Yes, you should know what to expect and prepare for it but the *situation* will indicate how you should tailor your response or choose not to respond.

Your response should depend specifically upon:

1. What is said
2. What the context is for what is said
3. What the other person's intention seems to be in what is said
4. To what degree their nonverbal behaviors match their spoken words
5. How important it is for you to choose to respond with either words or gestures

6. How useful it is to question, clarify, interpret, give feedback, confront, fog, or summarize what is being said to make sure you understand it
7. How you can benefit most by responding
8. When there appears to be no benefit in responding.

EXERCISE - *Actively Listening*

For your listening and responding to be effective, you need to communicate:

- I hear what you're saying
- I hear what you're feeling
- I understand how you see things
- I'm interested and/or concerned
- I don't judge or evaluate you as a person
- You don't have to be afraid of my censure for speaking out.

1. Have a conversation with a friend in your mind—make it someone with whom you feel comfortable. As you are conversing, make a point of doing the following:

- Step outside yourself, your thoughts and feelings
- Listen with interest
- Be open to what is said
- Respond with nodding and expressions of attention (e.g., "uh huh," "I see") to indicate you are hearing and understanding
- Absorb the content
- Actively grasp the facts and the feelings you hear
- Listen for total meaning (content and feeling)
- Note all subtle cues from the other's nonverbal behavior (body language)
- Sense underlying meaning
- Don't make assumptions or jump to conclusions
  Ask for clarification if necessary.

You'll need to repeat this process numerous times until you find you can walk and chew gum at the same time. It is normal and natural to tend to only half-listen and busy yourself with preparing your own response (or letting your mind wander to other things) instead of being aware of all the other is communicating. However, that tends to shut down the communication channel. You need to know how to keep that channel open with everyone, but especially with your boss.

2. Now have a conversation in real life with someone you know and with whom you feel comfortable. Make a point of following the active listening list of required behaviors.

3. In your mind have a conversation with your boss, making a point of following the active listening list of required behaviors above. Start small to see how it works for you. Now try something short and sweet in real life. Once you have done that, see yourself in your mind having a longer or more important conversation with your boss.

When you're ready, try something a little longer, perhaps a little more important, on your boss in real life. Keep building on what you accomplish and then expand it bit by little bit until you can feel comfortable and more confident talking with your boss.

Progress Report:
(Answer the following in detail)

1. What happened in your first attempt to listen actively in real life?
2. What did you do to step outside your own thoughts and feelings?
3. What facts and feelings did you learn?
4. What was the hardest thing to do to listen actively?
5. What assumptions or conclusions did you find yourself wanting to jump to before the other person had finished?
6. What nonverbal behaviors did you notice with the other person?
7. How important were the other person's nonverbal behaviors to your understanding of what the person was saying?
8. To what degree did you find you were able to get more from the conversation by actively listening?
9. Over the week what thinking and emotional differences have you noticed in what you have recorded in your log?

10. Make sure you recorded everything in your Daily Log.
11. Be sure to have spent several *days* on this designated section.

While you've received information on different aspects of how to interact with your boss throughout this course (but particularly in Stepping Stone III), there are other specifics you need to know about what to say and not say in speaking with your boss.

Because your boss has a position of status and authority, you need to show respect for that position. This means that unless you are asked to call your boss, or any other authority figure, by his or her first name, you should always use a more formal form of address: Ms./Mr./Mrs./Dr./Rev. plus Last Name. This may seem like common sense but to someone feeling intimidated by authority, it might not be.

You might hear colleagues refer to an authority figure by a first name or nickname and make the assumption that that is what to call the person. It's always better *never to assume* that that's the situation. If the boss does not tell you specifically how to refer to him or her, take the initiative to ask, "What do you want us to call you?" Or "How do you prefer to be addressed?"

Too many people simply assume they can call you by your first name whether they know you or not. Using one's title plus last name shows respect. Respect always creates a positive first impression. It also gives the other person the choice to say, "Call me ___."

In general, you need to speak to an authority figure in a more carefully structured way. Because people in authority tend to have to stick to schedules and have a lot on their minds, what you say to the person should take their time constraints into consideration. Therefore, ahead of time you should structure what you say to be as *brief* and *to the point* as possible while still covering the ground you need to cover. You want to tell your boss

- What you want to talk about—outline, leaving details until asked for
- What you see as important to share it with her—a problem
- What she cares/prefers to hear about—frame your subject in these terms
- Why you see it as important to the team—not just to you as an individual

- An example of why it is important—possible negative consequences of problem
- What suggestions you have about addressing it—approach or solution
- What the boss might want you to do toward resolving it, if anything
- How you'll respond to boss's suggestion, statement, or command.

Whenever you have a problem to discuss, no matter what the topic is, you need to express it in terms of *your* perspective. This is where you use *I-Messages*. That is, you say

- What you see is the problem ("When X happens, *I* see Y happening.")
- Why you see it as a problem ("When Y happens, *I* see it slow production.")
- How you feel about the problem ("*I* feel concerned when we can't get product out on schedule.")
- What you'd like or think could be done about it as a result ("*I* see one way to address the problem of X is to ___.")

This I-Message approach doesn't accuse anyone, including the boss, and gives no reason for the boss to feel defensive. When you use a You-message, the person tends to become defensive. Because of the implied accusation or criticism, they can become angry and the communication can stop abruptly. The person can no longer hear what you're really saying because he is wrapped in negative emotion, feeling attacked, and wanting to strike back.

When you present things to others in terms of *what you see, how you feel about it*, and *what you'd like done as a result*, it allows the other person to consider the problem as well as how to *act* to resolve it rather than *react* to its presentation and inferences. It is impersonal which helps keep the communication channels open and the information flowing.

Another aspect of speaking to authority figures is standing up for yourself. That is, if you disagree on something *important*, you should indicate, "I respectfully disagree about that," and then state why. If it is something minor, you can choose to speak up or say nothing about it. *Not every disagreement needs to be aired*. It depends on how important it is to you and to what degree you feel your self-esteem is involved.

The same goes for having a different point of view. If you feel that something is missing in a discussion or is not being addressed the way it needs to be, you can add, "I think it might be useful to also consider ____" and then add why.

Other things to remember when speaking with your boss:

1. Remain calm—never communicate when overwhelmed by emotion
2. Have a positive attitude
3. Be respectful
4. Speak for yourself only (I-Messages)
5. Keep out any anger, defensiveness, and personal attacks
6. Use the communication method the boss likes best, if it's not personal dialogue
7. Maintain comfortable eye contact (without staring) while speaking
8. Use a firm but pleasant voice
9. Don't hem and haw–just say what you need to
10. Don't sound humble, submissive, or groveling
11. Think "big picture"—why the boss should and will care about the issue which will generally be related to the company's bottom line in some way
12. Be brief, keep to the point—don't digress

13. Don't volunteer a lot of details—your boss will ask for them
14. Expect and be prepared for questions
15. Be prepared for possible disagreement
16. If your boss has any misconceptions or misunderstandings, correct them using I-Messages ("I believe I may not have stated that clearly. What I meant to say was ___.")
17. Communicate regularly with your boss but don't overwhelm her with trivia.

If you become friendly with your boss and see him in social situations, keep in mind that the social and the work situations are to be kept *separate*. You may be a friend in the social situation but you are a worker (and perceived "subordinate" or team member) in the work situation. This means you have to act (and are expected to act) accordingly in each situation. Keep in mind that you should *never* cross the personal-work boundary.

Also keep in mind that even in social situations you don't want your boss to see you doing anything that might reflect negatively on you. You don't want to get drunk or loud or obnoxious. You don't want to share secrets about your personal life or gossip about others in the workplace. You don't want to complain or whine. You and your boss may be friends but you are also in the perceived "subordinate-and-superior" roles. Thoughts, feelings, and impressions tend to flow freely from one situation to another so you need to keep your third eye open and aware so they don't.

If your boss in the workplace says, "Do it," it is incumbent upon you to respond positively and do it ... unless you have some moral, ethical, practical, or legal reason for not wanting to. It is not simply a matter of your not wanting to do it or having other preferences. This is your *boss* speaking, not your friend.

If, however, you have a serious reason for not wanting to, you have to explain what the problem is calmly and respectfully but know you may not get your way. Remember that you have contracted with the company to help them accomplish their goals *their* way. Unless there is a serious problem for you, you have to do it.

EXERCISE – *Speaking with Your Boss*

You practice speaking with your boss by creating scenarios based upon what you have already experienced, have seen others experience, or anticipate experiencing with your boss. In your Daily Log construct the first of your numerous speaking scenarios—as with the Empty Chair Exercise—using the following format:

- What the situation is
- What you want to or need to do
- What you will say
- How you will say it
- How your boss is likely to respond
- How you will respond to what your boss says
- How you will feel as a result
- How you will act as a result.

Go through the scenario in your mind, saying and doing what you feel is appropriate to the situation. Listen to yourself carefully. Does what you are saying flow like regular conversation? Even though you are writing this out first, this is not precisely how you will speak it. Writing tends to be more formal and less casual than how you would actually express it in a conversation. Listen to how you sound and rewrite what you want to say as you would speak it in small talk.

You need to practice this until you are comfortable with doing it. Then you need to create a visualization of your doing this, detailing precisely what you will say and how you will say it. This will make it more real and reinforcing. However, you are not trying to memorize what you are going to say. You are merely becoming comfortable with ways to flexibly present the subject. It's knowing the keywords that express the concepts you want to get across that count.

Once you are finished with your first conversational scenario, you then go on to the next scenario, following the same sequence. To make these scenarios stick in your mind and make them more likely to be available to you when you need them, you will need to go over them often, at least three (3) times a week.

Finally, you will look for opportunities to act out these scenarios, or ones like them, in your workplace with your boss. Start small by getting your boss's attention and creating a brief exchange. Then praise and reward yourself for each success and build on those. Look for opportunities to have more important interactions with your boss.

Each time you prepare by conversationally scripting what you need to say. If necessary, have notes with you to which to refer when you speak with your boss but *only* if the topic is serious or important. Otherwise, be more casual and speak off the cuff.

Final Progress Report: (Answer the following in detail)

1. Describe how you currently speak to your boss.
2. When do you currently speak to your boss—for what reasons or issues?
3. How does your boss prefer to receive most communications?
4. What things do you currently say to your boss when you approach her?
5. Describe how you outline the problem to your boss.
6. How do you demonstrate the importance of the problem as it relates to the team/task?
7. Describe how you present possible approaches and/or solutions to the problem.
8. How do you feel in these interactions?
9. What responses do you get from your boss?
10. What responses do you want from your boss you currently don't get?
11. What could you do to get preferred responses from your boss?

12. Describe the kinds of scenarios have you created. Do they fit most situations?
13. What happens when you act out your conversational scenario with your boss?
14. What does your acting out the scenario with your boss tell you about you and your boss?
15. Over the week what thinking and emotional differences have you noticed in what you have recorded in your log?
16. Make sure you recorded everything in your Daily Log.
17. Be sure to have spent several *days* on this designated section.

FINAL EXERCISE – *Your Overall Progress* (Answer in as much detail as you can)

Go back over ALL of your previous Progress Report responses (all weeks of your three Stepping Stones) in your Journal to see

1. How you answered those questions then and ask yourself how you would answer those same questions *now* that you have finished the course.
2. How your answers have changed over the course

3. How you would evaluate your current feelings about approaching, speaking to, and/or interacting with an authority figure.

STEPPING STONE III – SUMMARY

Stepping Stone III has shown you further ways to discover your self-worth, strengths, attributes, and confidence as a work contributor. It reminds you of the many ways you have been and can be and feel successful. It reminds you that you deserve to feel that way. Then it shows that to make your success confidence stick you need to praise and reward yourself—something which you have been unlikely to have been doing with any frequency before.

Stepping Stone III also addressed how to speak more confidently and competently with anyone but specifically with authority figures. With ready scripts you can know what to expect in interaction situations and be prepared with things to say. This relieves you of having to try to think up something on the spur of the moment—a situation which too often inspires anxiety, panic, and brain freeze.

The exercises in Step III as well as all the others in Steps I and II are designed to be used for anxiety in any type of social situation. This means that they are not only for fear of authority figures but also for any discomfort in any social situation.

For continued growth of your confidence in dealing with authority figures in the workplace, I strongly recommend that you keep up your Daily Log. That is, once you finish this course, you need to review all you have done over those weeks. Being comfortable interacting with authority figures is an ongoing process. This means that you will significantly benefit from continuing to practice and track your progress. Your Daily Log will still be an invaluable tool

You can be the successful, confident, savvy individual and worker you are. You can achieve what you want. And that's what it's all about. That's what Frank, Tasha, and Stefan discovered as they went through this course.

FRANK — Because Frank had low self-esteem, he struggled with the initial exercises about his strengths but toughed them out. He began to see his father and his own responses to his father as being behind his reluctance to assert himself with his boss. But it wasn't until he did the Empty Chair, that he was finally able to say what he wanted to his father who had morphed into his boss in his mind.

He now felt more like his "Hell's Angels"' image. He began by casually talking to all the workers on the assembly plant floor as part of a survey he had created. Then he reported his results to his boss. His boss's response was positive, thanking for his ingenuity.

TASHA — Tasha found she was having intermittent ahas! during the course. She saw that she had been caught in a conflict of "shoulds" and allegiances. She had given over most of her personal power to her minister who wanted her to be an activist. As a result, she was struggling to maintain what was left of her personal power and sense of worth to be the best computer design engineer she could be.

In her struggle, she couldn't deal with her boss who was a stand-in for her minister. When she saw authority figures simply as people with different roles and ways to accomplish them, she saw she could deal with the minister in her head differently.

Using visualizations, she saw how she could create more time to volunteer to do activism, which she considered important, and still be her professional self. She could make a proposal to her minister, one he could choose to accept or reject. That took her off the hook and gave her "permission" to talk to her boss.

STEFAN –When he discovered that all young interns went through hellish interactions with senior physicians, he felt a little less targeted and alone. He saw all interns being fired in the same crucible because of the physicians still abided by the old philosophy of "Since we went through this torture, they must too." Moreover, while those physicians did have a great deal of influence over the futures of interns, it was highly unlikely that an innocent question would precipitate a black mark on his record. Instead, it was mistakes with patients and medications he had to avoid because they had the potentially serious consequences.

Creating scripts for himself, watching the assertive behavior of more senior physicians, using his abdominal breathing, and doing role play, he was able to slowly, carefully approach his seniors. With practice he began to make suggestions and express his respectful disagreement. He even found a way to joke with the physician who stated Stefan wasn't capable of scooping elephant feces that he'd mastered that "scooping" art and had been graduated to "taking crap from physicians."

CONGRATULATIONS: COMPLETION!

§ § §

Congratulations on your completion of this course! You have smashed through your fear, tapped into your inner captain of your fate, and now can see yourself as stronger, wiser, and more the true master of the destiny you desire. Be sure to let me know about your progress.

If you have any other social fears you want to address, check out *Diagonally-Parked in a Parallel Universe: Working Through Social Anxiety* 2nd. Ed. in Paperback and Kindle.

If you need further assistance with your fear of speaking in any social situation, make small talk, or giving presentations, check out "How to Speak Without Fear Small Talk Course" also in Paperback and Kindle.

- Dr. Signe

drdayhoff@effectiveness-plus.com

ABOUT THE AUTHOR

§ § §

Signe A. Dayhoff, Ph.D., M.A., M.Ed., is a Social Psychologist with post-graduate training in counseling. She received her doctorate from Boston University. An authority on social anxiety and social effectiveness for the last 35 years, she has coached individuals internationally on overcoming fear and other obstacles, eliminating limiting thoughts and beliefs, and maximizing their strengths, skills, and confidence to achieve satisfying goals.

Currently she is president of Effectiveness-Plus LLC, which provides educational services and products. She is a Certified Graduate of Authentic Happiness [Positive Psychology] Coaching and is a member of International Coach Federation and International Association of Coaches.

Prior to this, she was president of The Mentoring Network, which provided mentoring and training in interpersonal skills for career development. She has taught psychology (general, social, and organizational) at Boston University, University of Massachusetts, and Framingham State College and has done research at Massachusetts Institute of Technology, Fairview State Hospital, and Scripps Clinic and Research Foundation. For four years she was producer/host of Continental Cablevision's alternate-career interview program, "The Inside Track," for which she received a Conti Award nomination.

She is author of 17 books: *Scared of Your Boss? Smash Through Your Fear Now; Promote Myself? I'd Rather Eat Worms!; How to Speak Without Fear Small Talk Course; 2nd Ed. of Diagonally-Parked in a Parallel Universe: Working Through Social Anxiety; What No One Has Told You: How Insiders Really Get Jobs; Create Your Own Career Opportunities; Get The Job You Want; How to Win in a Tough Job Market: Successful Strategies for Getting the Job You Want; Decision Making For Managers; Attracting and Dating the Wrong Men: Tips and Insights to Free Yourself; Growing Up "Unacceptable"—How Katharine Hepburn Rescued Me; Faust the Dancing Cat Does Vegas; Faust the Dancing Cat Tackles Strippers, Scammers & Bears; What Faust the Dancing Cat Taught Me; How Intrepid the Disabled Kitten Triumphed to Help Others; and Remarkable Tales of Cats Who Whisper to Humans.* She also contributed to David Riklan's *101 Great Ways to Improve Your Life (Vol. 2)* and Steven J. Bennett's *Executive Chess: Creative Problem Solving By 45 of America's Top Business Leaders and Thinkers.*

www.ingramcontent.com/pod-product-compliance
Lightning Source LLC
Chambersburg PA
CBHW060031210326
41520CB00009B/1085

* 9 7 8 0 9 9 8 5 3 2 4 2 4 *